TRUE SEXUALITY

TRUE
SEXUALITY

KEN UNGER

Tyndale House
Publishers, Inc.
Wheaton, Illinois

Scripture quotations are from the *New American
Standard Bible* unless otherwise indicated.

First printing, July 1987

Library of Congress Catalog Card Number 87-50278
ISBN 0-8423-7349-7
Printed in the United States of America

CONTENTS

It would be inappropriate for me to dedicate this book, my first literary effort, to anyone other than my wife, Barbara. Her constant, dependable love and understanding have released me to effectively serve in the ministry to which the Lord has called me. Without her loving support I never could have written this book; nor could I have ever become the father, pastor, and husband that I am today. I owe her my eternal thanks.

ACKNOWLEDGMENTS

There are many people without whose help this book could not have been written. First, of course, are my mother and father. They gave me the gift of life when they didn't have to and have always affirmed my right to be who I am. Next must come my grandparents, who provided for the education that prepared me for this task, and my Aunt Janis, who believed in me long before I did. After those, I must include Warren Campbell and Rob Reynolds. Their pastoral care has carried me through the times when I could walk no further by myself, and has enabled my character to grow in ways that wouldn't have been possible without their loving, gracious oversight.

Next I must commend, first among the typists, JoAnn Burton, whose devotion to the task and whose prayers and tears as well as typing enabled this book to become a reality. My secretary Karen Anderson, as well as Pat Shank, Barb Noble, and Brenda Hayes, offered tremendous help in this venture, as did Hazel Partington. Where would the church be without faithful women who are willing to serve the Lord in these kinds of thankless but essential ways?

In addition, I'd like to thank Peg Hartshorn, whose review of the manuscript offered some much-needed criticism and some desperately needed encouragement. I also want to acknowledge my friend Terry Truffin, who helped introduce me to my editor at Tyndale House. Terry's belief in me and his willingness to help in this way were invaluable.

Finally, I want to acknowledge and thank the people who are committed to our home church, Shalom Christian Fellowship. They have affirmed my writing gift and my calling, and unselfishly released me to do the will of God as I perceived it. I sometimes wonder what could be done for Christ's kindgom if there were more congregations like this one—people who share their pastor's vision and, rather than keeping him from pursuing it, assist him in fulfilling it.

INTRODUCTION

You will discover that *True Sexuality* is not a "how-to" sex manual, though the principles discussed herein—when understood and applied—can dramatically improve a person's sexual experiences. Yet neither is this a sex therapy handbook, though it does go a long way in defining sexual problems.

Instead, *True Sexuality* is an explanation of what God, the inventor of sex, says about how his gift of sexuality can best be used. The book is my attempt at a biblically integrated philosophy of sexuality that will help people understand the ways sex can enrich our lives.

To be clearly understood, our sexuality must be seen against the complex backdrop of society's attitudes, our purposes in life, our spirituality, our relationships with others, and the Creator's purpose and plan. That is why *True Sexuality* looks at sex holistically, emphasizing the relationship of one's sexuality to all of life and to the total person.

My hope is that this book will help Christians to understand, appreciate, and more adequately explain to others the Creator's wisdom on this vital subject. For too long we have talked about sex everywhere except in the places where people should be getting the best information—in the home and in our churches. It is time for that to change. I pray that *True Sexuality* will challenge parents, pastors, and teachers to explain the Creator's wisdom concerning our sexuality as it is revealed in Scripture. Today's liberal attitudes toward sex make it imperative for us to tell our children — and others — *why* God established specific guidelines and boundaries for our sexuality. Merely telling them *what* he says about these things is not sufficient.

When I was in high school and college I dealt with my sexuality according to my own rules with a dash of situation ethics added now and then. That route took me to the brink of abortion, impotence, and suicide. Then, when I became a Christian in my twenties, I began to discover the sharp contrast between the emptiness of sex outside of God's boundaries and the joyful fulfillment of my sexuality when God's guidelines were understood and followed.

That is why *True Sexuality* was written. The actual writing took seven years of struggle and rewriting. If the book helps one person see God's plan for his or her sexuality, it will be worth all of the effort.

Ken Unger
Box 214
Kingsville, OH 44048

PART I
Understandings:
Questions and Answers

ONE
SEARCH FOR UTOPIA

When I was an atheist, I justified my position by saying, "If there is a God, he would not allow the widespread human suffering we see everywhere around us." Similar sentiments prompted many of us in the late sixties and early seventies to begin a search for Utopia. Forsaking the shallow materialistic values of our parents' generation and the religious absolutes that appeared to be their foundation, we embarked on our own personal pilgrimage.

Our search was for a new life-style and a new set of values – an outlook that would help us understand and rectify the suffering and injustices we witnessed around us, and fill the cavernous emptiness within. We hoped that we could find our way back to a simple life-style, one that would satisfy both body and soul; one that would show us the way to inner peace and help us to discover and share the love we all so desperately needed.

Most of us abandoned the search far short of our goal. We became disillusioned by the strength and stubbornness of a greedy economic system, overwhelmed by the enormity of the task of renewing such a society. We were frightened and shocked by the extent of our own selfishness and the greed of those who plundered our naked vulnerability and made merchandise of our carnal cravings and desires. The majority of us gave up the quest. Some succumbed to their hopelessness permanently through suicide or

15

other forms of self-destruction. Others opted for the security of reclusive religious cults. Most merely capitulated to the selfish lifestyle that at one time had been so bitterly distasteful.

Today a few still cling to their utopian hopes. I am part of that fortunate minority. When I finally allowed myself to face the depth of my own inner emptiness, I realized that I would have to find what it would take to fill it or destroy myself in the process.

Henri Nouwen says the naive illusion of contemporary leadership is that people can be led out of the wilderness by those who have never been there. Unfortunately, I have been through more of the wilderness than I care to admit. But I am not so arrogant as to think that others will want to follow me into the Promised Land just because I am intimately acquainted with certain parts of the desert. Instead I would like to make this book an offering in the spirit of D. T. Niles. For him, evangelism—the sharing of God's Good News—is one beggar showing another where to find a crust of bread.

Though I consider myself a fellow pilgrim with you, I depart from Dr. Niles in this respect: I feel with all my heart that I've not just found a crust, but rather a perpetual feast.

WILDERNESS WANDERINGS

My personal wilderness wanderings plunged me into promiscuity. I lived in the slums of sensuality and found it to be a neighborhood that, though it appears otherwise, is not a pleasant place even to visit. Many others are discovering the same. Rollo May says that at one time people went to psychiatrists because they were sexually oppressed. They needed to be released from their guilt, they thought, so they could have and enjoy more sex. In today's society people seek clinical help because they experience more sex and enjoy it so little.[1]

This general trend in society is remarkable in light of a study commissioned several years ago by *Redbook*.[2] The study's conclusions were somewhat an embarrassment to the editors of that sophisticated women's journal.

The study was a survey of the relationship between one's religious commitments and sexual satisfaction. Naturally, given the accepted wisdom of our era, we logically would expect that the more religious a woman is, the less satisfactory her sex life would be. Astonishingly, the study showed the opposite to be true. The most sexually satisfied women in America are those with the strongest religious beliefs! In fact, there is a direct correlation between the extent of a woman's religious commitment and her satisfaction with sex.

The study also revealed that the most sexually liberated and un-"hung-up" women were the most dissatisfied and frustrated with their sexual experiences.

This study, had it been examined and adequately pursued, could have unearthed some surprising results. It could have led many people to acknowledge the obvious: that the Inventor of sex knows how it is designed to function. Sex as God intended it is far more pleasurable than sex as some people think it should be. In spite of our modern prejudices, the creator of sex still knows more about it than we do.

By the time I saw that study, I had already realized a profound scriptural truth. "There is a way which seemeth right unto a man, but the end thereof are the ways of death" (Prov. 14:12, KJV). I already had tried sex my way. My experimentation almost destroyed me and a few others. Doing "whatever feels good" led to a thoroughly exasperating experience of my own sexuality.

Someone once said that when all else fails, we should follow the instructions of our Maker. This is as true of sex as of anything. My own attempts to find sexual fulfillment led down the frightening path of promiscuity, uncontrollable compulsions, and finally impotence. It was only after discovering the wisdom of the Scriptures that I began to understand my own sexuality and to learn God's guidelines for enjoying sex.

I got into trouble over my own sexuality because the armchair theorizing that formed my sexual values was based on a disjointed view of life. I treated sex as an isolated experience, apart from the rest of my being. Sex was lifted out of context from the rest of my life.

To be understood, our sexuality needs be considered against the backdrop of society, our purpose in life, our spirituality, and the other relationships that are essential to our well-being. Any view of sex that neglects these facets of life cannot be considered truly holistic. Neither can it ultimately deal with the real source of our problems.

17

DISCOVERING ANSWERS

Prior to my conversion to Christianity, when I used the Lord as my scapegoat and the evils of our world as an excuse for my own unfaithfulness, I didn't realize how unjust I was in blaming God for the world's suffering.

Scripture reveals that God never wanted wars, disease, stealing, heartbreak, or violence. He placed our primeval parents in a garden paradise that came fully equipped. It was amply stocked with sufficient provisions to satisfy a person's every need for body, soul, and spirit. But it was man's own rebellion—the idea that he knew better than his Creator what would satisfy him—that caused him to lose that garden paradise.

Modern humans, even more than the ancients, believe that they know better than God how to satisfy their own needs and desires. Ironically, it is this mistaken assumption that is responsible for most human suffering. The greed and selfishness that cause us to use and harm our fellow humans are in direct conflict with God's will. Most human suffering is a consequence of our attempts to gratify our own desires without regard for how God intends us to live.

Our rebellion has caused much confusion and suffering in the arena of sexuality. The "new morality" has left in its wake many thousands of broken homes and wrecked marriages. It is responsible for more than one million abortions a year in the United States alone, and causes countless undesired pregnancies and loveless marriages. While an epidemic of venereal diseases ravage millions of bodies, guilt gnaws at millions of souls. Our psychiatric hospitals are full, due in part to unprecedented numbers seeking refuge in drugs, alcohol, and suicide.

In order to understand how man wandered off the path leading to abundant life and into this wilderness of depravity, let us turn our attention to the gospel of Sigmund Freud.

THE GOSPEL ACCORDING TO SIGMUND

Viennese-born Sigmund Freud (1856-1939), founder of psychoanalysis, lived in a time when religion had enormous authority over most people's lives. European and American society largely subscribed to the Judeo-Christian view of sexual morality. It appeared that science, however, was beginning to punch holes in the church's traditional view of reality. Christianity rapidly lost credibility in the eyes of many, especially the intellectuals. The church seemed incapable of showing people how its teachings could be integrated into their daily lives.

Lost was the understanding that biblical truth is true because it is God's Word about the best way to live. Many held that the teachings of the Bible were naive, outdated, and irrelevant. Science seemed to be a far more promising messiah than religion. Its doctrines were more comprehensible. Technical successes made science appear omnipotent. Besides, people were weary of obeying religious dogma and moral teachings they no longer understood or accepted.

The time was ripe for the atheist and scientist Sigmund Freud to expound a whole new gospel, one that would have almost universal appeal to people grown tired of religion and restless from its attempts to control their behavior.

Freud laid much of the groundwork for man's departure from a wholesome view of sexuality. While his more bizarre theories have been supplanted today, his erroneous assumptions concerning people's needs and behavior remain the cornerstone of secular society's "liberated" views. Many people, basing their ideas on Freudian theory, consider the source of their problems to be rooted in the repression of biological urges.

Later we will discuss in greater detail the specific errors inherent in Freudian theory. For now, it is sufficient to say that Freud's theories were inadequate because they were not holistic. As such they were incapable of treating the source of humanity's problems. They offered only superficial solutions that failed to satisfy deep inner needs. They neither took into account nor sought to minister to the totality of people's needs.

As an atheist and scientist who refused to believe in anything metaphysical (beyond the physical), Freud could treat only the symptoms of his patients. The life-style that has grown out of his theories exhorts us to pursue our physical impulses, but it does nothing to feed the hunger in our hearts. In fact, the scientific worldview most of us have been taught leaves us feeling more depersonalized, empty, and alienated than ever.

19

As Freud's time was ripe for him to seduce people away from their misunderstood traditional view of morality, today's time is ripe for a return to solid biblical principles.

Because science does not concern itself with the existence of spiritual reality, it can never assist us in the satisfaction of our spiritual quest. It is beyond the realm of science to help the individual find spiritural fulfillment.

It is also beyond the jurisdiction of science to reformulate the values we need to stem moral decay and avert the self-annihilation of our civilization. Morally, science can conclude only with the self-contradictory and absurd presumption that there are no absolutes. As we try to live with such freedom, we make self-defeating choices based on physical appetites and greed.

A WAY OUT

But there is good news. The Bible's premise is that we are made in the image of God. If this is correct, we can be assured of "finding ourselves" only by seeking to understand our Creator. Only the God who is Spirit can show us how to fill our inner emptiness; only he who created our world can teach us how to put it back together again. If we learn to live as he intended, we may yet avoid fulfilling the gloomy scenario that threatens our civilization.

It is crucial that we come to an accurate understanding of the God of the Bible. Humanity's rejection of God's ways is frequently the result of widespread misconceptions about his nature. One myth constantly perpetuated is that God is some sort of celestial killjoy bent on spoiling man's fun. This couldn't be farther from the truth. In fact, God is the creator of pleasure. He is also quick to remind us, however, that to live primarily for pleasure is counter-productive (Prov. 21:17). The same calloused conscience a person steadily develops as he wholeheartedly pursues pleasure also deadens his inner sensitivity to enjoyment. This eventually renders him incapable of finding real satisfaction or any joy in the fun he tries to have.

I used to think that God viewed sex as dirty, but a study of scriptural sexuality reveals that this just isn't true. God is the inventor of sex. He created it to be an earthly foretaste of the heavenly bliss that is the very essence of eternal life. God intended for sex to be intensely pleasurable. He wants us to be fulfilled in all ways. Jesus himself said that he came to give us the abundant life God had always promised his people (John 10:10).

If we are to comprehend how God's plan for our lives will fulfill us, it is essential that we understand his plan for creation. Only when we understand God's original plan for life and how he made us will we be able to realize where man went wrong. Only then can we stop being the enemy of our own well-being.

The lies about life that are destroying our society and causing so much personal suffering can be unraveled only as we understand God's truth. It has been said that earth is a marvelous planet whose only deficiency is that it came without an operator's manual. That's not accurate. The Bible is our operator's manual. Since all else has failed, it is time for us to follow the instructions of our Maker. After all, they were designed specifically to show us how best to live and love.

For us to do that, we must come to grips with certain scriptural teachings. What the Bible says about sex will make sense only when it is understood in relation to God's view of humanity and the rest of creation.

TWO
HEAVEN ON EARTH

An interesting fact about sex and other physical pleasures has been misunderstood by Freud and those who try to live by his philosophy. Because they do not comprehend this basic fact of life, they are not able to find the fulfillment they so desperately crave. Jesus states that fact clearly: "Man does not live [abundantly] on bread alone" (Matt. 4:4, NIV).

Because God is a spirit and we were created in his likeness and image, we have needs that transcend the physical—needs that must be met if we are to experience life fully. The fulfillment of these deeper needs brings about true self-actualization, inner harmony, and peace. Indeed, in the words of St. Augustine, "The heart of man is restless until it finds its rest in God." Because man is more than a mind and a body, mere physical gratification is insufficient to produce deep and lasting satisfaction.

Crucial to our understanding of ourselves is an understanding of the dual nature of creation. All of life begins to make sense when we realize that there are spiritual as well as physical realities, eternal as well as temporal values and principles. In order to understand life for the purpose of better understanding ourselves and God's provision for our well-being, let's turn our attention to Genesis, God's book of beginnings.

Genesis teaches that God created more than the earth. It teaches that he created *the heavens and the earth*. The unseen heavenly realities are every bit as real as the measurable earthly realities.

Any view of life and sexuality that emphasizes either heavenly or earthly reality to the exclusion of the other is destined to fail. Because secular approaches exclude eternal realities, they are incapable of ministering to people's deepest needs or solving their most perplexing problems. Similarly, religious solutions that emphasize the afterlife and fail to integrate eternal truth into daily living situations are irrelevant to the bulk of society. People need and deserve Scripture's practical answers for making their lives better and solving their daily problems.

A wholly biblical approach to life is sufficient for both the needs and the problems of mankind. Rather than being so heavenly minded that it is no earthly good, authentic biblical Christianity integrates the principles of heaven into the concrete situations of life. Its heavenly mindset is the very thing that makes it good for people of the earth. True Christianity brings the power and wisdom of the infinite to bear upon the problems and perplexities of the temporal world.

The reigning scientific worldview has failed because it provides only natural answers in response to man's needs. Scientific knowledge can improve the quantitative aspects of life profoundly. It can give us a shorter work week, make color televisions affordable, and help us more effectively fix people's broken bodies. It contributes little, however, to the qualitative facets of life. Science can neither heal our broken hearts nor fill our empty lives.

Only that which explores and explains life's ultimate purpose can give us a reason to live. Only the person who understands the principles of kingdom living set forth in God's Word can truly understand how to live this life to the fullest day by day.

Science captured people's hearts because traditional religious approaches often ignored their minds. Science has influence over our temporal destination. On the other hand, traditional religion has sometimes given us values that only moderately transform our priorities in this life. Because of its neglect or misunderstanding of heavenly realities, religion seldom has been of significant influence in conforming men's lives to the will of God. In many instances it has not been effective in integrating the principles of the Creator into people's everyday lives.

The secular world seeks to prepare people for *this* life, but it cannot provide them with a proven agenda for living fully. Neither can it offer them a reason to live. The church, on the other hand, has sought to prepare people for the *next* life, but it has seldom taught them how to thrive in this life or how to have much impact on the world. This is a far cry from the primitive church that turned civilization around in one century.

If we are to accurately comprehend the mysteries of our sexuality, we must lay groundwork with a scriptural understanding of the heaven and earth that God created. Comprehending eternal realities and integrating them fully into our temporal lives is a necessary prerequisite if we are to be made whole. The meaning and fulfillment of our sexuality come only to those who learn to live consistently with scriptural truth. That's because the Bible teaches the best way for us to live in accordance with who we are and to prepare us for who we are becoming. Only those who understand heavenly realities are equipped to live fully on earth. Heavenly facts, therefore, have profound significance for this life.

HEAVEN AND EARTH

In the Bible, heaven is the place where the Creator rules. It is his domain and the home base of his Spirit. Nothing happens there that is contrary to God's will. It is thoroughly yielded to his government. His eternal values dictate all behavior and policy. Heaven is a place of perfect harmony, love, and bliss, undefiled by human greed and selfishness. Consequently, there is no stealing or violence, no adultery or heartbreak, no pain, disease, or tears. Because it is the holy abode of him who is all-powerful love, there is none of the suffering caused by sin.

Earth, on the other hand, is where God's creatures rule. God gave humans not only freedom but also dominion over his creation. Ever since humanity asserted its own will in rebellion to God's and adopted predominantly temporal values, earth has been corrupted by sin and its consequences. Where people rule according to their selfish impulses, life is afflicted with the by-product, greed. Thus, earth is characterized by violence, war, hatred, envy, lust, disease, and strife – all things that cause pain and suffering.

According to the Bible, men and women were made to be filled with and motivated by the love of God. When they live contrary to

God's will, they seek to fulfill their internal emptiness through the gratification of their physical needs. Because this doesn't work, their needs become insatiable and their frustrations intensify. Because of greed God's heavenly garden on earth has turned into a temporal foretaste of hell.

After people do their dirty work with God's creation and begin to experience life's suffering, they usually turn an accusing eye toward heaven. *If God is good and all-powerful,* they wonder, *why is earth so bad and so ugly?* In ignorance, they blame humanity's mess on God, who has allowed people the freedom to choose how they will live. This is like the teenager who borrows his father's car, wraps it around a tree, injuring himself and others, and then says, "The accident is Dad's fault because he gave me the keys!"

How can we change the direction of our world? The answer is found in one of the most quoted portions of the Bible—the Lord's Prayer. In one familiar phrase is the key to unlocking God's provision for the needs of our world: "Thy kingdom come. Thy will be done in earth, as it is in heaven" (Matt. 6:10, KJV). It teaches that if we would see life on earth become heavenly, we must ask for the reign of his kingdom to be extended here. We must seek for his will to be done.

This prayer implies the inconsistency of saying we desire God's will but continuing to do the things that are clearly contrary to it. Herein lies a significant clue for our own lives. If we would partake of the benefits of God's abundance, we must live the way he wants us to. If we would purge our lives of the suffering that he never intended us to experience, we must exorcise from them the sin and rebellion that cause the suffering.

As individuals learn to live consistently with the principles of the heavenly kingdom, their earthly lives become richer and fuller. As they share the joy of this new way of living—of discovering how God intended for them to live and who they were created to be—they can help others to also discover the same keys to abundant life. Living by eternal heavenly values and thus extending further the reign of God's kingdom throughout the earth is what God meant for us to do with our lives. Herein is the key to making our own lives heavenly.

An understanding of heaven as well as the earth, as God created them, helps us find answers to the needs of individuals and society. Any attempt to change society without helping to make individuals whole is naive and doomed to failure. Empty, frustrated individuals without God tear apart society. Until the deepest needs of the individual are fulfilled, our world won't become a better place.

Likewise, any attempt to help individuals prepare spiritually for the next life without teaching them how to live and be whole in this earthly life is shallow and simplistic.

If the church would truly help men and society, it must be about the business of teaching men to integrate the eternal principles of God's kingdom into their daily, earthly existence. Only then can God's will be done and his kingdom come to earth. As men are taught to yield to the heavenly will on earth, men and society can be made better, both for this life and in preparation for the next. Anything less than this is sub-biblical, and will be inadequate to the challenge that confronts them. Any view of life that neglects heavenly realities only leads men deeper into the moral wilderness.

Only by integrating man's sexuality into an understanding of who he was created to be is man offered much hope of finding truly satisfying solutions to life's problems.

THREE
SCRIPTURAL LAWS
AND THE
GIFT OF GUILT

The sexual revolution of the sixties and seventies was precisely that. Traditional moral values and standards were almost completely overturned. In one decade, mainstream American society forsook its Judeo-Christian heritage to become what some theologians called a post-Christian culture. What made our civilization so ripe for this new morality and situation ethics?

I once believed that mankind had advanced so far we could now conclude that nothing was really right or wrong. I was convinced that all moral choices depended on one's individual situation. I knew nothing of the profound wisdom of Solomon who had proclaimed many centuries ago that there was nothing new under the sun (Eccles. 1:9). I was genuinely shocked, after my conversion, to learn that thousands of years ago, declining cultures also embraced an extremely individualistic morality. Shortly before each civilization crumbled, the Bible tells us, "everyone did what was right in his own eyes" (Judg. 21:25). I had thought that "do your own thing" was a new and enlightened philosophy that would lead to a better, happier, more holistic life-style.

The apostasy that caused ancient Israel's downfall was foreshadowed and cautioned against in the Book of Deuteronomy. An understanding of the purpose, context, and warnings of this amazing book of the Bible can similarly illumine us concerning the new morality of the sexual revolution.

THE PURPOSE OF THE LAW

Deuteronomy means, literally, "second law" or "repetition of the law." The first recital of the law began with the Ten Commandments. These were handed down to Moses shortly after Israel's deliverance from the pursuing Egyptians at the crossing of the Red Sea. The totality of the law was then summarized in Leviticus.

It is important to keep before us the purpose of God's law. The Lord told Moses to say to the Israelites, "If you will indeed obey My voice and keep My covenant, then you shall be My own possession among all the peoples, for all the earth is Mine; and you shall be to Me a kingdom of priests and a holy nation" (Exod. 19:5-6a). The word *holy* comes from a Hebrew root which means "separate" or "set apart." The people were to be both set apart *to* God, and separated *from* the things that would harm them. The Creator of the earth was seeking a people whom he could teach the best way to live. He didn't just want them to do his seemingly capricious will for his sake. He desired to show loving-kindness to thousands, to those who love him and keep his commandments (Exod. 20:6). Obedience was required of people for their own benefit.

It is also important that we understand God's motives. He loves all people. He never intended for humankind to be expelled from paradise, to experience death and suffering, or to be separated from the fullness of life he provided for us. He had given humans free will, however, and their abuse of that freedom caused them to sin and cut themselves off from God, the source of all true wisdom concerning creation. Consequently, humankind blunders through life, blinded by "the deceitfulness of sin," going from bad to worse, killing, stealing, and being killed and robbed. But because he loves us, God sought to devise a way to reestablish his benevolent rule over our lives and thus protect us from ourselves.

That opportunity was afforded through the miraculous deliverance of the Israelites from the hands of the Egyptians. The Lord seemed to reason that if he could reveal his love, power, and majesty to these broken and enslaved people, he could earn their trust. If he could then bestow upon them his wisdom through laws that would show them the best way to live, they would begin to obey him. Through that obedience, God's creatures would experience the blessedness of living consistently with the true nature of his creation. He could lead them safely through the wilderness, and restore them to a land of abundance similar to the garden paradise they had forfeited in the Fall.

Through pouring out his loving-kindness and generous provision on an obedient people, he could use the witness of his love for Israel as a glorious magnet. That nation's blessed existence would stand out in vivid contrast to the cursedness of the lives of the lost nations surrounding it, and lift up the Creator as the source from whom all blessings do truly flow. God's goodness toward the Israelites could then capture the attention of those nations and draw them again to submit to his benevolent reign over their lives. As the pagan people could see and respond to God's goodness, his redemptive purposes could be performed. At least that was how the Creator's reconciliation with his creatures could have been accomplished.

But before Moses came down from Mount Sinai with the original tablets of the law, his impatient people had turned to worshiping idols and cavorting drunkenly in the countryside. Unfortunately, this was but a foretaste of their rebellious wilderness wanderings.

The wilderness was a proving grounds to test the obedience of God's people (Deut. 8:2). They had said they would do whatever the Lord told them. God, however, has always had a realistic appraisal of our good intentions. He knew that though the Promised Land was filled with abundant blessings, it was also packed with peril. The wicked Canaanites, whom the Jews would have to displace, and the wild beasts who occupied the land were too strong for people with lives dissipated by sin. Only people who had learned to conquer their own appetites would be adequate to the task of overcoming such powerful adversaries. Only people whose might and fulfillment were rooted in God would be sufficiently strong and confident to seize and hold the blessed land of promise.

Therefore, all evil, rebellion, and sin had to be purged from God's people before they could enter into Canaan. Otherwise, the people could easily be seduced by the abominable practices of the very people God sent them to destroy. God's righteous rule would not be established, and his plan for redeeming mankind from the cruel curses of sin could be thwarted.

WHAT'S WRONG WITH IMMORALITY?

At this point, before we examine the message of Deuteronomy and its implications for apostate America, we would do well to consider the sins of the Canaanites and examine why God felt it essential to destroy his enemies completely.

Leviticus 18 catalogs the sins of both the Egyptians, who had enslaved the Jews in the past, and the Canaanites, whose sins, if practiced by God's people, would ultimately destroy them. Most of the sins listed were of a sexual nature. Familial nudity, incest, adultery, and homosexuality were all mentioned and categorically condemned. Such practices were considered wicked, not because God didn't want his people to enjoy sex, but God never intended what he created to be corrupted and used for immoral purposes. He knew that fulfilling their lusts would only frustrate the people and bring additional problems, eventually causing the downfall of their civilization.

When sex is "desacralized," in the words of the famous secular psychologist Abraham Maslow: "More and more exotic, artificial, striving 'techniques' may escalate further and further until they become *necessary* [emphasis his] and until jadedness and impotence ensue . . . stronger and stronger stimuli are needed to produce the same response."[1]

As a punishment for these sins the land itself would spew out its inhabitants (Lev. 18:25). It would also spew out the Israelites or any other people who neglected God's mandates and defiled the land with this kind of activity (vv. 26-28). Notice that it is the land itself, not God, that casts out the Canaanites.

Though the laws of God run counter to man's carnal inclinations, tainted and deceived as they are by original sin, his mandates are thoroughly consistent with the laws of nature. In fact, when God warns us to avoid something, it is always because he has our best interests in mind. He is concerned with our highest good.

The Lord enjoined his people to "not practice any of the abominable customs which have been practiced before you, so as not to defile yourselves with them" (vs. 30). God is more concerned with what our sins will do to us than what they will do to him. He labeled unclean only those things that had the potential to harm the people he loved.

The word *defile* was used to describe anything that was "ritually" or medically contagious. Impure practices could easily spread contagious diseases and even cause death. God's warnings concerning uncleanness served as an "effective quarantine for public health."[2]

The same laws of God that effectively protected the ancient Jews from disease and death form the cornerstone of our own culture's modern health practices and are largely responsible for the phenomenal success and well-being of Western civilization.

Neglect of these regulations is likewise largely responsible for the disease and depravity of many societies. Evidence of this can be found in India and primitive cultures not founded upon the wisdom of Judeo-Christian laws.

The close proximity of our excretory and sex organs probably led to the unfortunate belief that sex is unclean. The elimination of bodily waste can lead to uncleanness, hence our emphasis on cleanliness in this area. Nothing in the Bible, however, teaches that sex is unclean in itself. God pronounced his creation good, not evil. Ironically, the snickering approach to sex modeled by the secular media and comedians contributes far more to that misconception than does the church.

Man can also be defiled emotionally, intellectually, and spiritually. Moral disease, though far more subtle and difficult to recognize than physical, can be equally devastating to the well-being of a society and its members.

But sexual impurity is especially dangerous. Because of its capacity to give intense pleasure it also has a powerful potential to destroy people. Familial nudity can easily lead to incest. It is devastating to children and other family relationships. Adultery often leaves women with young children who are vulnerable and uncared for, subject to privation and abusive men. The women themselves become inwardly bruised and heartbroken.

Homosexuality is called a hateful abomination. It is destructive to family life, fueling unnatural lusts that can never be satisfied, encouraging a particular variety of crippling emotional and sensual selfishness. Such practices are hateful (not hated) because they are especially devastating to people's self-esteem, causing them to hate themselves, which in turn often fills them with hatred toward others.

A study of the implications of the word *abomination* is informative. Those who commit abominable deeds become "loathsome, detestable." They are "sure to bring God's wrath" upon them.[3]

Because these deeds are unnatural and inevitably corrosive to one's well-being, God has built within us a protective guilt mechanism to steer us away from them. *Pure guilt is to the soul what pain is to the body.* It's an early warning system to steer us clear of things that would defile us. Guilt can be ignored, causing our hearts to become calloused and our consciences seared and rendered incapable of feeling guilty when they should.

It is dangerous to allow rationalizations to bypass the protective warning system given by our loving Creator. Guilt warns us of God's displeasure. Because guilt reflects God's judgment upon our sin, it has a profound effect on our self-esteem. How can we feel good about ourselves when deep inside we know that God is unhappy with what we are doing?*

The lower a person's self-esteem, the higher the self-hatred level rises and the more vulnerable he or she becomes to pursuing the temporary comfort offered by the immoral deeds that caused the problems initially. Unless something intervenes to break this cycle, the downward spiral continues with the individual's life going from bad to worse.

A person's problems profoundly affect and infect society. Sin causes heartbreak. Without repentance this usually leads to more sin and the inevitable deterioration of family life. All of this encourages the spread of disease, inner agony, and crimes of passion, hopelessly complicating the problems of society.

Productivity is ultimately affected. People soon have no way to sustain themselves, leading to more crimes, of passion at first and later of necessity for survival's sake. History demonstrates that an entire civilization can self-destruct by feeding on the immorality within itself. Disease, depravity, death, and disintegration eventually bring about its downfall.

History also seems to teach that a civilization can reach a point of no return, after which it is impossible for a people to be restored through repentance. This happens when sin's deceit stops people's ears and blinds their eyes. Their crimes against nature and one another cause innocent people to suffer without cause. Neighboring

---

*Though many behavioral scientists tell us we should never feel guilty, the astronomical problems we face concerning our low self-esteem are directly related to our departure from solid moral values. These problems can never be cured by the platitudes of the secular psychologist.

lands and peoples become polluted with their corruption. Violence, disease, and suffering become the norm.

At this point it may be more merciful for a people to be wiped out completely than for their agony to be prolonged. The innocent, if there are any, will fare better at the hands of a just God on the far side of eternity than they could ever manage in this life at the hands of their fellowman.

Such was the situation in Canaan as God was preparing to lead his people in to displace its perverted occupants. It was in light of this that the deuteronomic warning became significant. Remember, God was speaking to the offspring of the people he had led out of Egypt. Their parents' generation had died in the wilderness, never having been allowed to enter the Promised Land because of its unwillingness to obey the Lord. Now those children, untainted by distorted memories of Egypt, purged of their rebellion by the wilderness and toughened by its trials, were preparing to cross the Jordan and conquer Canaan.

The Lord reminded them first of the purpose of his commandments: "And now, O Israel, listen to the statutes and the judgments which I am teaching you to perform, in order that you may live and go in and take possession of the land which the Lord, the God of your fathers, is giving you" (Deut. 4:1). These were no arbitrary regulations. Obedience was essential for their very lives. The possibility of victory, the promise of abundance, depended on it.

> You shall not add to the word which I am commanding you, nor take away from it, that you may keep the commandments of the Lord your God which I command you. Your eyes have seen what the Lord has done in the case of Baal-peor, for all the men who followed Baal-peor, the Lord your God has destroyed them from among you. But you who held fast to the Lord your God are alive today, every one of you. (vv. 2-4)

At first glance we might wonder if these verses or the laws of the Old Testament or even the New Testament have any relevance for us today. In modern America, are there any reasons why the biblical restrictions on sexuality should speak with clarity and meaning to us today?

If we consider the realities around us, we find that the standards governing the ancients in their search for a Land of Promise are the same for those of us today who seek a better life. There are those whose misfortunes are directly attributable to their disobedience of God's commands and stand as a vivid warning concerning the perils of moral pollution today.

I think of the astronomical suicide rate of teenagers and wonder how many of those tragic deaths are related to the abuse of sex, lack of self-esteem, or an overwhelming sense of guilt. I think of my own friends who have suffered from divorce or drug and alcohol addiction in a vain attempt to anesthetize their guilt. I am reminded of an estimated 20 million homosexuals in America, many of whom have given up hope of changing. Finally, but certainly not least in significance, are the over 1.5 million unborn babies sacrificed annually through abortion to the American idols of convenience and selfishness.

Consider the suffering of the mothers, fathers, children, grandparents, and friends of people with these life-styles. There is no such thing as a sin that hurts no one. At best, sin hurts the sinner.

Deuteronomy's warnings about sexual immorality and the laws of both the Old and New Testaments pertaining to scriptural sexuality are profoundly relevant for today's people.

FOUR
IMMORALITY:
INNER EMPTINESS
WITH NO BOUNDARIES

Few people, it would appear, are aware of their own inner emptiness. Those who are aware usually have a difficult time understanding why they feel frustrated and unfulfilled—why, deep within, they feel so empty.

The majority of Americans possess many of the things our world says a person needs to be happy and to enjoy relatively good health. While their own family life may not be as happy as they would like, neither is it seriously troubled. Even if no crucial problems are currently assailing their lives, there are vague but persistent feelings of incompleteness. Something important is missing. When Peggy Lee sings "Is That All There Is?" many may hope someone will shout an emphatic no and point the way to something better; but somehow that never happens. Without knowing what is amiss, they find it impossible to discover a solution.

When war, hunger, disease, poverty, and ignorance stalk a civilization, it is easy for citizens to assume that peace and education will bring utopia. A culture with such problems may have the delusion that exorcising its society of these particular economic and social ills will guarantee happiness. When, however, a civilization finally conquers most of its external enemies, it faces a much tougher problem—driving out the inner enemies within the hearts of its citizens, such as selfishness, greed, or hatred. No civilization has yet mastered this feat. Many nations have disintegrated because of their inability to do so.

If Western civilization is to outlive its painful phase of cultural adolescence, if it is to continue to grow and not be consumed from within by the moral cancer that has brought the collapse of other civilizations, it must discover how to satisfy the thirsty souls of its populace. Society can thrive only if its individuals fulfill God's purpose for their lives.

Civilization is like a living organism whose cells are its individual members. When the health of the individual cells is threatened, the whole body is in danger of extinction. Conversely, when each cell prospers, the whole body functions well. Genesis 1:2 provides a clue as to what is sapping the vitality of the individual cells of our society. The chaotic condition of the earth at its early stage of development is analogous to the upheaval and confusion so prevalent in the lives of many individuals. The verse states that the earth was without form, and void (empty). In fact, its emptiness was a direct result of its lack of form.

God had a definite plan for his creation, but at this stage it was not realized. For the earth to be filled with the life and beauty he intended it to have, for it to fulfill God's purpose, it had to be given the proper form. Without having the proper form, the earth was incapable of being what God planned for it to be.

Contemporary humanity's problems and potentials are similar to the earliest stages of earth. The inner void people experience is real. But God intends for life to be richer and more significant than what most people experience. Modern humanity's crisis is one of form. Only by finding the scriptural "form" will men's lives conform to the shape God intended for them. Only by accepting and conforming to God's boundaries will they find it possible to fill life with beauty and meaning.

In *The Wounded Healer* Henri Nouwen describes a young man whose confusion over forms typifies that of so many individuals in late twentieth-century western culture. Describing this bright, handsome, yet empty man of twenty-six, Nouwen says this:

> As we talk, it becomes clear that Peter feels as if the many boundaries that give structure to life are becoming increasingly vague. His life seems a drifting over which he has no control, a life determined by many known and unknown factors in his surroundings. The clear distinction between himself and his milieu is gone and he feels that his ideas and

feelings are not really his; rather, they are brought upon him. Sometimes he wonders: "What is fantasy and what is reality?" Often he has the strange feeling that small devils enter his head and create a painful and anxious confusion. He also does not know whom he can trust and whom not, what he shall do and what not, why to say yes to one and no to another. The many distinctions between good and bad, ugly and beautiful, attractive and repulsive, are losing meaning for him. Even to the most bizarre suggestions he says: "Why not? Why not try something I have never tried? Why not have a new experience, good or bad?"

In the absence of clear boundaries between himself and his milieu, between fantasy and reality, between what to do and what to avoid, it seems that Peter has become a prisoner of the now, caught in the present without meaningful connections with his past or future. When he goes home he feels he enters a world which has become alien to him. The words his parents use, their questions and concerns, their aspirations and worries, seem to belong to another world, with another language and another mood. When he looks into his future everything becomes one big blur, an impenetrable cloud. He finds no answers to questions about why he lives and where he is heading. Peter is not working hard to reach a goal, he does not look forward to the fulfillment of a great desire, nor does he expect that something great or important is going to happen. He looks into empty space and is sure of only one thing: If there is anything worthwhile in life, it must be here and now.[1]

OUR SCHIZOPHRENIC SOCIETY

This crisis of form and boundaries, of being unable to discern right and wrong or even be convinced that such distinctions are relevant today, has affected our generation. Herman Hesse makes an allusion to our cultural confusion in *Steppenwolf*, his penetrating study of the dual natures of exalted humanity and vicious beastliness that uncomfortably coexist in every person and so painfully manifest themselves in the schizophrenia of modern humanity. Harry Haller, Hesse's wolf of the Steppes, speculates:

A man of the Middle Ages would detest the whole mode of our present-day life as something far more than horrible, far more than barbarous. Every age, every culture, every custom and tradition has its own character, its own weakness and its own strength, its beauties and ugliness; accepts certain sufferings as matters of course; puts up patiently with certain evils. Human life is reduced to real suffering, to hell, only when two ages, two cultures and religions overlap. A man of the Classical Age who had to live in medieval times would suffocate miserably just as a savage does in the midst of our civilization. Now there are times when a whole generation is caught in this way between two ages, two modes of life, with the consequence that it loses all power to understand itself and has no standard, no security, no simple acquiescence. Naturally, everyone does not feel this equally strongly. A nature such as Nietzsche's had to suffer our present ills more than a generation in advance. What he had to go through alone and misunderstood, thousands suffer today.[2]

Whether or not Hesse's compassion for Nietzsche is justified, his insights into the sufferings of modern humanity and culture are valuable.

Individuals and society as a whole suffer because an entire generation is straddling two opposing views of life and is unable to decide which to follow. Many progressive people would have us reject the values once held by our forefathers and launch out into the uncharted waters of a different set of values. The vague, new lifestyle has no unifying philosophy, no recognizable boundaries. Paradoxically, its only absolute is relativity, its only goal is the elusive hope of personal fulfillment and freedom, its only concern the gratification of selfish desires.

The philosophy of "every man doing what is right in his own eyes" is not a new life-style. It is as old as humanity. The results of such a philosophy have always been devastating. Not only does such an approach to life inhibit an individual's quest for real fulfillment in life, but it also destroys a culture.

It is no wonder this trend causes so much pain and confusion in society. The word *schizophrenic* is derived from the Greek word *schizoid*, which basically means being torn apart as a result of going in two different directions at once. This is the dilemma not only of many individuals but also of much of our society.

Most people are reluctant to relinquish their individual right to do whatever feels good. At the same time, most people sense the difference between right and wrong – the values of the past. The inner confusion, stress, and anxiety of such a hypocritical position pull individuals apart from within and alienate various parts of our culture from others. Unless a way can be found out of this dilemma and onto a more solid foundation of values, Western civilization will destroy itself out of sheer frustration.

Why have so many people chosen to reject the Christian values on which our nation was founded?

BIBLICAL FORMS AND MEANING FOR LIFE

Today many people seek escape from the frustrations of thinking about life because they don't understand where we've been as a culture or where they individually should be going. Our world provides many cerebral anesthetics to dull the brain against the confusion of society. Drugs, alcohol, and illicit sexuality are some of the obvious vehicles for escape. Some less obvious ones are compulsive work habits, overeating, television, sleeping too much, and just general busyness. Even religious practices can provide some addictive sanctuary. Khalil Gibran was right: "You talk when you cease to be at peace with your thoughts."[3] Or, we worship one of our familiar gods – the idol with whom we are likely to find the most comfort, the one who is most capable of drowning out our thoughts. If that god is also capable of inflicting some deserved chastisement on our tortured psyche, and so helps to atone for our inner feelings of self-loathing and unworthiness, so much the better.

We try to escape because we don't know how else to cope. Frequently, our teachers, pastors, and parents have been unable to help us understand what has been happening and how to cope with life. Often, they themselves haven't known. Modern philosophy lies mortally wounded, with one consequence being that there are few metaphysicians around to heal our tortured souls. Even many spiritual leaders have had to seek help in their own personal diversions – to immerse themselves in the familiar haunts of the ivory towers of intellectualism, and overwork, and play that really isn't fun.

By understanding the changes that have pummeled our civilization, we can better equip ourselves to decide which way to go with our own lives. But probably only a few will understand (Matt. 7:13-14). The masses of our world will continue careening toward an oblivion they sense is impending, but about which they don't know what to do. Most will continue to search for larger and deeper sandpiles in which to bury their heads.

All this is unfortunate, because the Bible gives clear guidance on the question of colliding cultures. Though ours may indeed be the last to be rent asunder by its own inner confusion, it is certainly not the first. Understanding the past can protect us from being condemned to repeat it. That's where the Bible can help us the most, and that's largely why it was written.

GOD'S INTENTIONS AND PROMISES

We have talked about the fact that God intended for people to occupy a garden paradise and that it was their refusal to trust God's wisdom that got them expelled. What we have not discussed is that it has always been God's will for us to be restored to that garden. No one wants to help us get back to that garden more than God does.

To that end he brought about the deliverance of the Israelites from their Egyptian bondage in the land of sin as told in the Book of Exodus. God led the Israelites out into the wilderness with the promise of a new garden paradise:

> I will bring you out from under the burdens of the Egyptians, and I will rid you out of their bondage . . . and I will take you to me for a people, and I will be to you a God: . . . and I will bring you in unto the land, concerning the which I did swear to give it to Abraham, to Isaac, and to Jacob; and I will give it to you for an heritage: I am the Lord. (Exod. 6:6-8, KJV)

God promised the land would be flowing with milk and honey. So rich and lush would the land be that the honeycombs would literally flow with honey, the cows would effortlessly give their milk.

Deuteronomy is the second recital of God's law. Through it God hoped to teach the people how they must live in order to conquer, subdue, and retain the land he had promised them. Here God again describes the substance of his promised abundance. He also issues an urgent warning, one that has profound implications for us. Let's consider it again:

> And it shall be, when the Lord thy God shall have brought thee into the land which he sware unto thy fathers, to Abraham, to Isaac, and to Jacob, to give thee great and goodly cities, which thou buildest not, and houses full of all good things, which thou filledst not, and wells digged, which thou diggedst not, vineyards and olive trees, which thou plantedst not; when thou shalt have eaten and be full; then beware lest thou forget the Lord, which brought thee forth out of the land of Egypt, from the house of bondage. (Deut. 6:10-12, KJV)

Like Eden of old, the Promised Land would come complete. God promised to provide lavishly for his people's needs and leave them sufficient leisure to enjoy him and their blessings. God knew, however, that it was at just such a time that the people he blessed would be most vulnerable.

Isn't that how it is with us today? It's not the hard times that push me away from God. I am never so close to him as when I need him most. Rather, the good times estrange me from my Maker. It's when he has bailed me out of my problems and things are running smoothly that I am in the most peril. If I'm not careful, I forget about God, except in the most perfunctory ways. I am tempted to go on about my business, and soon drift back into the very sins and stubborn habits that caused my suffering.

In Old Testament times the Sodomite culture was notorious for the extent of its depravity. Ezekiel had this amazing insight into the roots of Sodom's sins. They were: "pride, fulness of bread, and abundance of idleness . . . neither did she strengthen the hand of the poor and needy" (Ezek. 16:49, KJV). Those were the underlying sins that precipitated the destruction of an entire society. Everything was going well for the Sodomites. Their needs were amply provided. They had plenty of leisure time. But, rather than invest that time in helping the needy, they gave themselves to selfish gratification. This same danger that caused the destruction of Sodom now threatened Israel if they failed to heed God's warning. The same dangers threaten America today. That's why the rise of the "me generation" forebodes so much ill for our culture.

THE ROOT OF MAN'S PROBLEM

To comprehend the significance of a passage like Ezekiel 16:49 we need to return to the Genesis narrative concerning the fall of humanity. There we find the core of people's problems. If we can understand what Genesis subtly reveals to us to be the source of our human dilemma, we can then find a way to genuinely gratify our deepest individual needs. Only then can we discover solutions to our sexuality that are fulfilling and satisfactory.

Whether one believes, as I do, that the Genesis narrative is literally true, or chooses instead to ponder it for figurative significance, he cannot deny that it has much to teach us about God, humanity, and the roots of our problems. Genesis 2:7, 15, and 16 tell us much about human nature, what destroys our well-being and why we have the problems we have. This information is essential to those who would seek lasting solutions for humanity's problems and satisfaction for our deepest needs.

> The Lord God formed man [Hebrew for man is *adam*] of dust from the ground [Hebrew for ground is *adamah*], and breathed into his nostrils the breath of life; and man became a living being. . . . Then the Lord God took the man and put him into the garden of Eden to cultivate it and keep it. And the Lord God commanded the man, saying, "From any tree of the garden you may eat freely; but from the tree of the knowledge of good and evil you shall not eat, for in the day that you eat from it you shall surely die." (Gen. 2:7, 15-17)

These statements teach us much about our nature. Human beings are more than merely a product of the earth. We are more than the chemical substance of our body parts. The Greek word used for breath here is the same as the word used for spirit. We are thus spirit and body, a combination of dust and divinity. What makes us living beings (literally "living souls") is the union of the spirit of God with earth's clay. That is why God is called the Lord of life. His breath, the very spirit of the living God, is what gives and sustains life.

What is the significance of this? For now let's be aware of two things. First, the core of our being—our soul, our true self (another way to describe the soul)—is inextricably related to our Creator. Since science has not yet found a way to quantitatively measure or record the spiritual realm, it can do very little to solve our root problems. Spiritual discernment and wisdom are necessary if real problem-solving is to occur. Such wisdom is a rare phenomenon (1 Cor. 1-3).

A second insight to be gleaned from this passage is found in the unavoidable consequences of our disobedience. The Lord said that *in the day* man would eat from the tree of the knowledge of good and evil he would die. The inevitable effect of rebellion against the Lord of life is death. Or is it? Certainly death and all its ugly consequences entered the world, but did Adam and Eve die, as God said they would, on the day they disobeyed? Either the God of the Bible is wrong here, or we are working with an inadequate definition of death.

I opt for the latter. Many years passed before the physical death of Adam and Eve took place, but that physical death was only the final outworking of something initiated on the day of the Fall. Adam and Eve became spiritually dead the day they turned from the wisdom of their benevolent Lord and began to partake of their own knowledge of good and evil.

Again I say: "There is a way which seemeth right unto a man, but the end thereof are the ways of death" (Prov. 14:12, KJV). That's why Jesus, God's second Adam (1 Cor. 15:45-47), would be required to visit earth centuries later. He came to enable whoever would receive him and yield to his lordship to be born again (John 1:12; 3:3-6). The Apostle Paul later revealed to us that we are all dead (not dying) in our own transgressions (Col. 2:13) before Christ gives us a new life through the regeneration available through the Spirit of God (Titus 3:5-6).

At this point a person may well wonder what all of this has to do with sexuality. This information, however, is crucial to our understanding of man's deepest needs. Unless those needs are truly filled, we shall seek to satisfy ourselves in ways that lead only to further frustration and deprivation.

God made us for himself. He who created us intended to fill us with himself. Our inner emptiness is a spiritual void. Nothing material can fill it. No amount of sensual pleasure, possessions, or creature comforts can satisfy the deepest yearnings of the human heart. Those who fail to understand that may destroy themselves in the pursuit of pleasure. To be certain, many have. True satisfaction belongs to the spiritually discerning, those whom Jesus said had "eyes to see." Those who have eyes but see not will go to their graves having experienced a mere shadow of the blessedness that could have been theirs.

The root of our problem lies in our inner void. As long as this "God-shaped vacuum" remains unfilled, our own inner insatiability will be our undoing. No amount of sanctified selfishness will help us find fulfillment; no amount of sensual indulgence will satisfy. Is it any wonder the "me generation" has such a voracious appetite for pleasure?

Our situation is frightfully similar to that of the Sodomites. Like them, we also have "pride, fulness of bread, and abundance of idleness." We too have failed to love and obey God and give ourselves to selflessly serving the poor and needy; our exasperating sexual excesses are the decadent result.

Like the Laodicean church mentioned in the Book of Revelation, we think ourselves to be rich, wealthy, and in "need of nothing," when in fact we are "wretched, and miserable, and poor, and blind, and naked."

PART II
Issues:
Understandings in Action

FIVE
ISRAEL AND AMERICA:
PARALLEL LANDS
OF PROMISE

The parallels between ancient Israel and modern America are sobering. Just as the oppressed Israelites looked forward to a good life in the Promised Land, the Pilgrims, who had been religiously and socially oppressed, eagerly set sail for a land of promise — America. Like Israel, America was founded by people who looked forward to living in a nation under God. Both the Israelites and the early Americans faced cruel hardships and an abundance of tribulations that caused them to cling to God in utter dependence.

During the 1700s a European statesman visiting colonial America returned to his homeland to report that he had discovered the key to America's strength, greatness, and increasing prosperity. It was, he announced, the uncompromising righteousness extolled from the pulpits, a righteousness that showed God's people how to tame the wilderness within their hearts, thus enabling them to subdue their hostile environment.

God's Word to the Israelites as they prepared to move in and receive the land promised to their patriarchs was clear:

> Ye shall diligently keep the commandments of the Lord your God, and his testimonies, and his statutes, which he hath commanded thee. And thou shalt do that which is right and good in the sight of the Lord: [As usual, he even tells them why they must obey him.] that it may be well with thee, and that thou mayest go in and possess the good land which the

Lord sware unto thy fathers, to cast out all thine enemies from before thee, as the Lord hath spoken. (Deut. 6:17-19, KJV)

The Lord went on to tell the Israelites that they must utterly destroy their enemies and break all their altars. While this seems quite brutal, it really makes sense. Remember, as we discussed earlier, God was displacing these pagan nations because of their abominations. Refusing to worship the true God, they had chosen instead to consort with lifeless and pagan idols. To appease these gods, the nations had gone even so far as to sacrifice their own children. (Our idols in modern America seem to be exacting the same price from us. Is not obedience to the shrines of luxury, beauty, pleasure, and comfort destroying the lives of many unborn as well as living children?) No, God was not unjust in destroying these pagan nations, nor would he be unjust in allowing our destruction should we fail to repent.

The Israelites finally did begin to conquer Canaan. Nation by nation, God miraculously delivered Israel's foes into their hands. As life got easier for the Israelites, though, they became lax in obeying his commandments. As self-righteous people often do, they tried to be more loving and tolerant than God. They left in their midst remnants of the Canaanites and their idols—remnants that would soon become the unrighteous leaven that eventually polluted God's people, requiring that they who were once the dispossessors would become dispossessed.

As with Israel, so also with America. Most recently, after World War II, we too became proud and prosperous. Modern technology left us with more time on our hands. An abundance of idleness together with our rich blessings became our undoing. As the post-war baby-boom children grew up, they became the first generation in America to receive "vineyards they'd not planted, houses they'd not built," and abundance for which they had not had to labor. Christian principles succeeded for us so well that the majority of our people finally had the wherewithal to provide for their basic needs and many luxuries as well as plenteous leisure . . . but soon forgot from whose hand it had come. Science and technology convinced us that we didn't need God. Perhaps our own depravity and unsolvable problems will reveal to us how wrong we were.

PAVING THE ROAD TO HELL

If we are to understand at this point the differences between the two generations that collided in the sixties and did so much to alter the course of our culture, it is necessary to glean some insights from a psychological theory called "need hierarchy." John Powell concisely describes this theory:

> The late and great psychologist Abraham Maslow saw us in pursuit of our human goals and needs according to a definite hierarchy: a ladder with many rungs. The lower rungs of the ladder are the fundamental drives for food, shelter, safety from external threats. The middle rungs are the more precisely human set of needs and goals—the "higher order" needs of dignity, belongingness, love. At the summit of Maslow's ladder are the highest human aspirations: independence and excellence. He calls this state "self-actualization."[1]

In a sense, the concept of need hierarchy merely explains the dynamics of covetousness. We all have basic needs and struggle to see that those needs are met. We think that if only we didn't have to be concerned with our next meal, or the roof over our head, or clothes, we could be happy. Once all these basic needs are provided for, however, we find our heart desiring not just a home, but a lovely home; not just a meal, but a gourmet dinner. As we achieve more and more of our desires, our wants expand. Eventually, our desire is no longer directed outward toward things and external fulfillment. Instead, our focus turns inward toward emotional, self-actualizing, interpersonal satisfaction. We become more concerned with being than with having.

That person or generation whose basic and medium-level needs have been provided for perceives higher needs that clamor for attention—needs rooted more deeply in the soul than in the body. If such a person also has time on his hands, he or she begins to ask ultimate questions in the search for identity and happiness. Fuel all of this with an approach to education that has taught us to accept nothing on someone else's authority, to challenge and question all the "traditional" methods, and it's easy to see why the sixties were so morally combustible.

Most of the people who lived through the Great Depression and

World War II had been taught to conform to traditional values. They went to church, believed in America and hard work, and generally accepted society's Christian concensus and values. After World War II, many Americans came to the decision that they would "give our kids what we never had." And they were keenly disappointed and befuddled when their children rejected their sacrifices along with their religion and traditional values.

These parents didn't realize that the possessions and security they cherished, the things that were so important to them because they'd been denied them in their youth, were not important to their children. Because their children had never been without the food and clothes and comforts they wanted, they had grown up with "higher order" needs than those of their parents. Just as their parents grew up regarding automobiles, TVs, and carpeting as needs rather than luxuries, so these baby-boom children grew up taking for granted the luxuries for which their parents had labored. They felt that they had deep, inner, personal needs that had not been fulfilled.

How many parents have felt the exasperation of working long, hard hours to provide nice homes, automobiles, and education for their families only to hear their adolescent children say, "You never loved me!" The frustration of both parent and child is understandable.

Parents labored to give their children what they themselves would have wanted. In so doing, they were "doing unto others what they would have them do unto them." They were loving their children as well as they knew how, but the children didn't feel that their needs were understood or served. The parents worked hard, but they didn't provide for their children's *felt* needs. Often the hard work and long hours made it impossible for Mom and Dad to provide the personal attention and affection their children craved.

As materialistic desires were intensified by the propaganda on television, the burning desire for a "close, loving family" was stoked by unrealistic television serials that made children feel that other parents really loved their kids. I remember watching "The Andy Griffith Show" and wishing my father would knock off a day and take me fishing. Who didn't long for the understanding father that Fred McMurray represented in "My Three Sons"? Who hasn't envied the concerned involvement of the "Brady Bunch" or the "Eight Is Enough" family? Unfortunately, the intimacy and depth of caring reflected in these programs were a vivid contrast to the hurried superficiality of most families and marriages.

Once these postwar baby-boom children reached adolescence, a whole new youth-oriented culture began to prey on their vulnerable minds and affection-starved souls. Barbie dolls and portable radios enticed children barely out of kindergarten toward dreams of teenage sophistication, glamour, and excitement. Teachers who'd been trained in increasingly humanistic institutions began introducing existential values—values rooted wholly in the here and now that promoted immediate gratification of drives and desires rather than eternal principles. These valueless standards sought to supplant the traditional Christian consensus but failed to replace it with anything workable.

Young people were encouraged to find themselves instead of God; to be true to their own feelings and opinions instead of God's revelation in the Scriptures; to follow their hearts instead of their heads; to live for their own gratification instead of assuming responsibility for their neighbor's well-being. No wonder they have had problems relating to other people.

It is easy to understand how these new ideas could have been so attractive. Christianity's success was also its downfall. Living by the principles and values of Christianity had done much to eradicate disease, ignorance, and poverty, yet it made us so safe and comfortable that we no longer felt we needed God. We began to believe we could handle things well by ourselves.

The story is told of a man who, while fixing his roof, lost his grip and began to slide down its sloped side. Unable to stop himself, he cried out to God for help, whereupon his trousers caught on a nail and prevented his plunge to certain injury or death. Scrambling back to security, he called out flippantly to the heavens, "Thanks, God. I can take it from here."

So has gone the history of our nation. In gravest peril, we have clung closest to God and his ways. Once we attained that measure of comfort and safety—the inevitable reward of putting aside the unclean things that pollute our hearts and bodies—we decided we no longer needed God.

THE CHURCH'S COMPLICITY

Though we have lived by Christian principles and received the rewards of virtue, America as a whole has not truly known God in a profound way. Though we have prided ourselves on being a Christian nation, we have, in fact, been a nation of people who had an outward form of righteousness – a surface conformity to Christian values and principles – but none of the inner substance that integrates the outer form with a heart understanding of what life is all about.

God has no grandchildren. Each generation of people must be born again and become children of God directly. If they aren't, they will become like the whitewashed sepulchers that Jesus condemned: clean on the outside, but inwardly every bit as polluted as the cold, sin-hardened people who make no pretense of righteousness (Matt. 23:23-28).

Many young people who went through adolescence in the sixties and early seventies grew up with parents who went to church more out of habit than conviction, who blindly advocated Christian virtues they often didn't understand and couldn't explain. They thought that being nice was synonymous with being Christian and had little understanding of the essence of the gospel or the implications of discipleship.

During this time there were largely three dominant approaches to religion. None of them was equipped to serve the "higher order" needs of this new rebellious generation. None was capable of coping adequately with the tumultuous changes that with tremendous success would alter the entire value structure of our culture.

One kind of church was rigid and dogmatic. Children were taught to do things a certain way because "God would get them" if they didn't. When the children went off to secular colleges or began to reason for themselves, this approach became increasingly suspect or distasteful to them. As the influence of culture moved farther away from the values they'd been coerced into believing, they rebelled against their childhood faith. Without a reasonable understanding of right and wrong and the strength to formulate and defend their own convictions, these young people gradually drifted away from the dogmatisms of their youth, often becoming hostile toward anything resembling the repressive religion that had been thrust upon them.

2.

A second approach, characteristic of mainline Protestantism, was the corporate social involvement approach—the so-called secularization of the church. Youth were encouraged to see the Christian faith in terms of making sacrifices to help deprived groups of people in concrete ways. These young people, however, often felt somewhat lost in the depersonalized maze of mass society. Hungering for the personal attention their parents didn't give them, yearning for ways to discover who they were and how to find personal fulfillment and solid values, they were exhorted to help the oppressed. They were told that people can't hear the gospel while hungry; but often they were told this by people who were unaware of the spiritual vacuum in the hearts of their young audience. Ironically, the starvation of souls these youths experienced made it impossible for them to obey gospel imperatives themselves.

3. The third group was taught to see the gospel as having only spiritual implications for life. Getting saved meant living a religious existence in this life in order to attain to some uncertain heavenly reward. Little was taught concerning the relevance of scriptural principles to an earthly life. Naturally, as people embraced the religion of modern science and were less able to believe in something as intangible as the hereafter, they found their faith unable to withstand the doubts that assailed them.

None of these options meant much to a generation whose inner hunger and quest required that they find a faith that was nurturing, relevant, and comprehensible.

All in all, though adherence to Christian principles had brought prosperity, health, and many of the advantages that minimized human suffering and labor, those same values have become the scapegoat for the very things many people see as being wrong with society. Because Christianity taught us, for our own good, to control our carnal appetites, many now see Christian values as the cause of problems such as guilt and repression. Because Christianity taught us to rule our spirits (Prov. 25:28), there are those who came to see it as the force responsible for the emotionally frigid environment in which many people were raised.

As our world continues to embrace non-Christian values involving fornication, adultery, homosexuality, drug abuse, abortion, and materialistic and hedonistic pursuits, Christianity will be seen as the one thing standing in the way of people's fulfillment. It will become both more hated and more loved as society polarizes. It will be seen as the enemy of the state, human potential, and the self-enslavement that passes itself off today as liberation.

LIFE WITHOUT BOUNDARIES: THE PERILS OF MORAL RELATIVITY

The life-style of the church seemed sterile and pallid in comparison to the gospel of personal fulfillment peddled by the existentialists. Is it any wonder the world turned away? The old wineskin of traditionally moral churchianity of the fifties seemed so passé. When the evangelists of situation ethics told us there were no absolutes, we were ready to swallow it, hook, line, and sinker. Certainly "do your own thing" seemed to be the best way to find oneself and be happy. Few could anticipate the perils of this philosophy or the havoc that raw, unchained human emotions and behavior would cause to society and its individual members.

When liberalism led people to believe that humanity was basically good, who could have ever dreamed that lowering a few moral fences would flood our culture with pornography, or that making it possible for women to receive abortions on demand would end up costing the lives of more than 1.5 million unborn babies a year? Who would have expected when we did away with capital punishment that the homicide rate would skyrocket as it has, or when we allowed pornography to flourish that rape, domestic violence, and incest would increase so dramatically? And these have led to teenage drug and alcohol problems that destroy so many lives and an escalating suicide rate among teenagers. Didn't the experts assure us these things wouldn't happen? Aren't they still fumbling for ways to explain our bent toward violence? Some believe that the violence we experience as a culture is a by-product of the excessive boredom that grows out of living for pleasure and without purpose.

We should have expected some of these things. So often the wisdom of this world proves to be foolishness (1 Cor. 1:20-21, 25-29; 2:12-16; 3:18-20). Authorities made absurd statements so often that we began to believe them.

Probably the most naive statement is the one that started (or at least gave tremendous impetus to) society's moral erosion—the theory that everything is relative and there are no absolutes. The application of the theory of relativity to morality has caused our modern crisis and plunged society into moral and ethical chaos.

The theory of moral relativity arrived on the scene just at the point when Americans were most bored with relatively problem-free lives. At the same time, the liberal social theorists were on their own witch-hunt to discover why there were such things as racial injustice and the napalming of innocents during the Vietnam War. To these naive idealists the answer did not lie in humankind's fallen and sinful nature. Believing that people were basically good, they had to look elsewhere for the source of evil. A logical place was in the structure of society. Since our society was founded upon Christian principles, it was only reasonable for them to assume that these absolutes must be causing the problem. It was felt that if we could be free from rigid moral restraints and the alleged repression they caused, our own inherent goodness would make the world a better place. People would finally be able to live happy and peaceful lives.

Anyone who stopped to think about this would see how absurd these conclusions were. How could a fence be responsible for letting the sheep out unless it was broken? These people, far from advocating that we fix our fences, were naive enough to suggest that if we take down all the fences the sheep won't run away and the wolves won't plunder.

We who should have seen through this fallacious reasoning were instead so ready to sample the harvest beyond our own fences that any excuse to do so became adequate. When Joseph Fletcher's *Situation Ethics* was published, we were already tired of religious expressions that absolutized everything and made us feel guilty for drinking, using an occasional swear word, or doing anything that seemed fun. So when someone offered us an intellectual key to unlock the moral gates, we were all too ready to storm the fences and force our way out toward all those lush, greener fields that always seemed to beckon us from the other side. Little did we know that God's fences were as much to keep our enemies out as they were to keep us in. How quickly we forgot that they had been built by a loving heavenly Father who only desired to protect us from our own fallen, misguided instincts.

The very statement that there are no absolutes is a flagrant contradiction in terms. It is the same as saying, "There are absolutely no absolutes." In so doing, we disprove our own theory by making an absolute statement!

Even if this theory were intellectually cohesive, everything in life teaches us that it is false. To be certain, there are absolutes in the physical world. Try to act as if the law of gravity isn't always the same, or as if some people can swallow poison and not be affected by it. If there is a difference between toadstools and mushrooms in the physical world, what makes us think there is no deadly poison in the moral universe?

Do we really know what it means to say there are no absolutes? I would like to hear someone justify rape, or incest, or murder (not killing, murder). See if you can convince anyone that these sins are relative. Explain how rape or child abuse are justifiable.

We are free moral beings, created to have a free will. We choose our own behavior based on what we believe to be right and wrong, good and bad. Programming a whole generation to believe that nothing is wrong, that people should be able to do whatever they want, is akin to putting matches into the hands of children and leaving them untended.

This was brought home to me some years ago when I ran a coffee-house ministry at Geneva-on-the-Lake, Ohio. Often I would dialogue with young people about biblical views of right and wrong. On more than one occasion, I was shocked to learn how extensively the concepts of situation ethics had taken hold. In one particular conversation, a small group of middle-class young adults told me they thought there was nothing wrong with killing someone to take from that person something you wanted. I began to see why moral erosion could cause the downfall of a civilization.

There *are* absolutes. To say there aren't is, first of all, intellectually absurd. Second, it is contrary to all that the rest of life teaches us. Finally, to say there are no absolutes is to turn a blind eye to the things that threaten to destroy each of us from within and unravel the fiber of civilized life.

Since we cannot with any wisdom or integrity say there are no absolutes, it then becomes our task to decide just what absolutes there are. What moral choices always precipitate suffering? What can we never do, without hurting someone? Which paths are there that, if taken, almost certainly lead to the erosion of the quality of our lives and perhaps even to the destruction of life itself?

It is here that the Bible can be a real help. It lists very few absolutes, but its lists are quite inclusive. Few, if any, of the things it condemns could be argued by any reasonable and informed person to be relatively harmless, either to individuals or to society. In a few half-dozen passages the New Testament lists those sins that will keep us from inheriting God's kingdom (Rom. 1:29-32; 1 Cor. 6:9-10; 2 Cor. 12:20–13:5; Gal. 5:19-21; 1 John 5:16-17; Rev. 21:7-8).

THE KINGDOM WITHIN

As we consider these passages, it is essential that we understand what is meant by the phrase "inherit the kingdom."

God's will from the beginning of time has been that people should be heirs to a garden paradise. Even after humankind relinquished the rights to that paradise, God sought to reestablish people in a new land of promise. God, the Creator of all that is of value and worth in the universe, chose to relate to them as a heavenly parent, intent upon helping them inherit his promised abundance and blessings.

When the ancient Israelites persistently refused to live in such a way as to empower themselves to conquer and retain Canaan, God's earthly land of promise, the Lord sent his Son to earth to give abundant life (John 10:10). God, through Christ, ushered in his kingdom and taught any who had ears to hear how to inherit that kingdom. Christ came to make them joint heirs with him in the inheritance of his Father's kingdom (Heb. 9:15). He came that they might become his brothers and sisters.

It is important for us to realize that the kingdom of God is to the New Testament what the land of Canaan was to the Old: the fulfillment of God's promised abundance. God's kingdom is the inheritance that he wants his children to receive (Luke 12:32). It is important to underscore these biblical teachings because unless we understand the kingdom of God biblically, we will perpetuate the errors made by so many who envision it only as an after-death inheritance or a politically attainable human ideal.

Jesus taught that the kingdom of God is both eternal and internal; that it is relevant to this life, as well as to the afterlife. According to Jesus, God's kingdom is within and among us (Luke 17:21). We need not experience physical death to receive the kingdom's blessings. All we have to do is to accept Christ's teachings and die to our own willful selfishness (John 12:24-25). The kingdom of God can be entered and enjoyed by any who will allow God to be their king.

All that is necessary to begin inheriting God's kingdom is to enthrone Christ as king of our own personal lives; to allow his will to govern our lives (John 6:35-40). Through letting Christ rule over our choices, we can have our cake and eat it, too. We partake in the blessings of his eternal kingdom in this life as well as in the next, receiving the just deserts of being a member of God's family.

It is vitally important that we have this understanding of God's kingdom. When Scripture teaches that those who become beset by certain sins will not inherit the kingdom of God, it does not only mean that they will go to hell. Those who become hopelessly ensnared in sin also consign themselves to a living hell on earth.

When the Bible teaches that Jesus is the way, the truth, and the life (John 14:6), it informs us that following Christ is the best way to get the most out of life. Contrary to the common caricature, Christianity does not require us to adhere to a lot of irrelevant rules designed to insulate us from anything that would make life enjoyable. The kingdom of God produces righteousness, the fruit of which is peace and joy in communion with the Holy Spirit (Rom. 14:17).

Because God loves broken sinners, he hates the sin that broke them. And because he desires for us to inherit the blessed life, which is a by-product of obeying him, he warns us against sin.

God calls sin anything that separates man from God. All biblical laws and principles lead to a joyous and pleasurable existence; but sin promises a fulfillment it cannot provide. Someone has said sin is a promising employer, but a poor paymaster. C. S. Lewis said that sin offers an ever-decreasing return in exchange for an ever-increasing investment. This is what is meant by Isaiah's pleading invitation:

> Ho, every one that thirsteth, come ye to the waters, and he that hath no money; come ye, buy, and eat, yea, come, buy wine and milk without money and without price. Wherefore do ye spend money for that which is not bread? and your labour for that which satisfieth not? hearken diligently unto

me, and eat ye that which is good, and let your soul delight itself in fatness. (Isa. 55:1-2, KJV)

Sin is often an attempt to fulfill our inner spiritual needs through outer physical pleasure. As such, it is self-defeating. Disobedience to God's commands can never enrich our lives. Instead, sin destroys us through enslavement to insatiable lusts. This leaves us physically frustrated, emotionally drained, and spiritually debilitated. We either feel guilty or emotionally frigid because we have hardened our hearts against guilt, and, in the process, sealed ourselves off from all tender emotions as well.

God's Word gives us moral boundaries. These are the ethical forms we need to avoid the chaos that comes when we seek fulfillment through a totally free-form existence.

Even a football game requires rules and boundaries to ensure the safety of the participants and maximum enjoyment of the sport. How much more necessary, then, are boundaries and rules in real life? Traffic without stop signs is dangerous and foolhardy.

Through conforming our lives to the boundaries established in the Scriptures, through heeding God's warnings about sins, our lives can become filled with all the beauty of life that God intended for his children. His boundaries help us learn to live life more fully than just for the superficial pleasure of indulging our biological whims. Through Christ we become heirs of God's kingdom and so live according to the depth of life that his Holy Spirit enables us to perceive and enjoy. We experience the joy and peace of his abiding presence.

Thus the prodigal forsakes his or her spiritual poverty and returns to the inner mansions provided by a loving and benevolent heavenly Father. The unspeakably incredible bonus the prodigal also receives is the promise of living in God's eternal heavenly paradise. That means finding the way back to the garden both now and forever.

SIX
FREUDIAN FALLACIES

Alienation is felt as a loss of the capacity to be intimately personal. . . . We go to bed because we cannot hear each other; we go to bed because we are too shy to look in each other's eyes, and in bed one can turn away one's head. . . . [1]

It should not be surprising that a revolt is occurring against the mores which people think cause alienation; a defiance of social norms which promise virtue without trying, sex without risk, wisdom without struggle, luxury without effort – all provided that they agree to settle for love without passion, and soon even without feeling.[2]

People who have had all of their immediate needs met, who have been handed cuisine, clothing, new cars, and sufficient leisure to face themselves and begin the long journey inward – the search for one's true self – soon discover the real cost of inherited luxury: it is usually the loss of one's identity, initiative, and sense of worth. It can easily lead to the loss of one's true self. In the quest to recover these things, other inner yearnings become too evident to ignore. As people face their own impoverishment of spirit, two things often happen. First, they discover how desperately they need love, acceptance, and fulfillment. Second, they become angry with the society whose values deceived them into believing they were rich when in fact they were mere paupers spiritually.

Our own society is beginning to realize the bankruptcy of the value system we inherited from Freud. Evidence of this is found in books such as *The End of Sex* by George Leonard and *The Culture of Narcissism* by Christopher Lasch. This generation, like Freud's, has become disillusioned with the mores of our traditional Judeo-Christian heritage. If neither of these alternatives worked, one wonders what philosophical framework would lead us to a deeper sense of satisfaction.

If we are to find authentic satisfaction, both for our sexual needs and for the deeper parts of our being, we must explore the Freudian fallacies that led to the contemporary view of sexuality. Unless we accurately appraise the failure of Freudian values, our society will probably take another philosophical detour that can only lead to further alienation, dehumanization, and frustration.

Freud's alternative to the Judeo-Christian value structure was quite appealing to many. Within forty years it seduced the imagination of a whole generation, enabling people to scornfully cast off the "Victorian shackles" of the previous age. Freud sought to help people deal with the emotional blockage that kept their psyches imprisoned in various neurotic and psychotic behavior patterns. As he talked with disturbed people, he rightly understood the paralyzing power of their own guilt. As an atheistic materialist he wrongly diagnosed the source of that guilt. Because Freud did not believe in anything nonmaterial, he could not understand that guilt is a spiritual and moral reality. He assumed that all guilt was psychological—totally a product of one's social and religious conditioning.

Freud believed that society was bent upon subverting the fulfillment and well-being of the individual for the sake of civilization. To him, our culture assumed that the "free gratification of man's instinctual needs is incompatible with civilized society. . . . Happiness must be subordinated to the discipline of work as full-time occupation, to the discipline of monogamic reproduction, to the established system of law and order."[3]

As a naturalist Freud believed that if people were free to do the things that gave them pleasure, they would be happy. He rightly understood the curse of earning one's bread by the sweat of his brow (Gen. 3:17-19). He also recognized civilized society's need to sublimate the uncontrolled gratification of individual needs. Without that, there are not only many problems, but there is also a probability that the energy needed to work for the common good would be hopelessly dissipated by sensual pursuits. However, Freud failed to understand how the best interests of the *individual* as well as society are advanced by the proper channeling of the individual's desires and needs for pleasure.

Freud believed that social constraints worked against people's capacity to gratify their needs for pleasure, keeping them from realizing their fullest human potential. Thus they were robbed of their ability to find fulfillment. Freud rightly understood that a person would have to undergo a fundamental transformation to be free to pursue happiness, but he misunderstood the nature of that transformation.

Instead of seeing a person's need to change his or her center of reference from self to God and others, Freud believed that the person would have to change his or her own value system. He would have to adopt a new standard for living that would enable him to ignore guilt and do the things that would give him pleasure. Freud ultimately rejected the view that the individual must change. Instead he believed that our whole society would have to change. Only then, he surmised, could people be free to do the things that would lead to true happiness.

Freud saw a "pleasure principle" at work within individuals. If allowed to function freely, this instinct was supposed to lead to happiness and fulfillment through the gratification of each person's natural desires. This conflicted with society's civilizing efforts, which he called the "reality principle."

It is obvious that Freud's view of the source of our happiness was based on another factor. Besides being an atheist and materialist, Freud was also a male. It is highly doubtful, were he female, that he would have measured personal happiness with the superficial yardstick of sensual gratification. As reported in *Christianity Today*, a *Cosmopolitan* magazine survey of 106,000 women showed that the majority of women were disillusioned with the emotional fruit of the sexual revolution. The survey indicated that a sexual counterrevolution may be underway. Many readers expressed a deep longing for "vanished intimacy, and the now elusive joys of romance and commitments."[4] To most women, love and sex have never been and never will be synonymous.

Freud's promised salvation through sensuality didn't work, and its failure became evident to him before he died. In his middle and later writings "he began to see that the gratifying of the sexual drive itself—the full satisfaction of libido with its reduction of tension—has an ultimately self-defeating character and tends toward death."[5]

Freud realized that "our instincts, which seem to propel us onward, are now only moving us in a great circle which is doomed to come back to death."[6] He who sows to the flesh shall reap of the flesh corruption (Rom. 8:6). The wages of such sin are death (Rom. 6:23) because abuse of our God-given freedom enslaves our bodies to that which can never satisfy (Isa. 55:1-7), that which is in fact subtly self-destructive (Gal. 5:16-25). Had he been well-versed in Scripture, Freud could have discovered this much earlier in life, without leading modern civilization so far astray.

When Freud realized that libidinous sexuality led to death, he turned his philosophy to eros.[7] This alternative is understandable but equally erroneous. Because of the subtlety of its deception, it has only led society to one more dead end, still farther away from wholesome and truly redemptive truth.

Historically, eros is not synonymous with eroticism and sensuality; this is a modern misunderstanding. In Greek mythology, Eros was the god who created life on earth. Augustine saw eros as the power that drove men toward God. To be sure, for many people the desire for the sensations of romantic love have opened them to God. For Roman Catholics, marriage is a sign of God's love for us. The mystics often described their love for God in ways analogous to human passion.

Rollo May vividly explains the physiological distinction. He says of sex and eros:

> Sex . . . [is the] building up of bodily tensions and then release. Eros, in contrast, is the experiencing of the personal intentions and meanings of the act. Whereas sex is a rhythm of stimulus and response, eros is a state of being. The pleasure in sex is described by Freud and others as the reduction of tension; in eros, on the contrary, we wish not to be released from the excitement but rather to hang on to it, to bask in it, and even to increase it. The end toward which sex points is gratification and relaxation, whereas eros is a desiring, longing, a forever reaching out, seeking to expand.[8]

The Greeks saw eros as something that included but also transcended romantic love:

> [It was] the drive toward union with what we belong to—union with our own possibilities, union with significant other persons in our world in relation to whom we discover our own self-fulfillment. Eros is the yearning in man which leads him to dedicate himself to seeking *arete*, the noble and good life. . . . It is this urge for union with the partner that is the occasion for human tenderness. For eros—not sex as such—is the source of tenderness. Eros is the longing to establish union, full relationship.[9]

To Christians—those who have made Jesus their Lord and yielded their lives to his Spirit—it is easy to understand why this new twist in Freud's understanding of love was just as inadequate a solution to humankind's needs as his earlier emphasis on sex.

Love is the opposite of death; Freud was right to assume that. It alone can conquer death *(thanatos)*, but human love alone is inadequate for this task. Even Freud saw that in a person's own strength, his reservoir of love is painfully finite. Freud stated that "when a person loves someone else there is a depletion of the love he has for himself."[10] There is a need for a love that cannot be depleted—one that leads to a healthy sense of self-love and transcends our human limitation.

It's no wonder there's so much disillusionment and despair in our world today. People have followed Freud on his pilgrimage and have fallen for the modern masculine myth that sensuality satisfies. This often leads to venereal disease, rejection, unwanted pregnancies, guilt, homosexuality, impotence, or emotional frigidity. Ironically, it has not provided the promised fulfillment.

When people finally see the futility of trying to fill their emptiness with sensuality, they often turn to a more feminine solution, the desire for romance *(eros)*. But romance cannot satisfy our deepest needs either. The reason is simple: No human being can fill the vacuum in his or her life that is reserved for God alone. All human love is insufficient for humanity's most profound needs.

Henri Nouwen stated this quite remarkably in his book *Clowning in Rome*. In effect he said that if we suppose any person can fulfill our deepest needs, we will be severely frustrated.

When we expect a friend or lover to be able to take away our deepest pain, we expect from him or her something that cannot be given by human beings. No human being can understand us fully, no human being can offer constant affection, no human being can enter into the core of our being and heal our deepest brokenness. When we forget that and expect from others more than they can give, we will be quickly disillusioned; for when we do not receive what we expect, we easily become resentful, bitter, revengeful, and even violent.[11]

The devastating disappointment of the failure of romantic love can lead to even deeper problems than frustration over the failure of sex. Heartbreak and loneliness hurt far worse than physical suffering. The feelings of self-hatred and alienation that cascade upon a person who has been divorced or romantically shattered can lead to a form of despair that plunges him into violent acts against himself or others. Drug, alcohol, and food abuse, as well as insatiable greed and compulsive work habits, can all be used to escape the pain resulting from romantic failures.

Freud's fallacies have not led us into the Promised Land. Indeed, because we have followed him, we have been looking for love in all the wrong places. Neither sensuality nor emotional love alone can save us. What can? Let us now consider God's divine design.

SEVEN
THE DIVINE DESIGN

Someone once wisely said, "To be or not to be; that is not the question. *How* to be; that is the question." In our "existentially enlightened" era, life's most important questions are how and why, and the relevance of these questions spills into the sexual arena. Secular deliberations over sexuality have led much of society astray because behavioral scientists fail to ask *why* before they seek to teach us *how*. The end result is a mindless approach to sex that has caused a beautiful experience to become empty, commonplace, and meaningless for many. "So much sex and so little meaning and even fun in it!"[1] It is ironic, pitiful, how little we enjoy our emancipation, for it has cost so many so much.

Attempts to recapture the mystery and exuberance that should permeate good sex often have led only to its further debasement. Until we can fully discern God's purpose in creating sex we shall be unable to engage in it meaningfully. That which was intended to be an unspeakable blessing will continue to be a frustrating and mystifying enigma.

If we are to find our way out of the moral wilderness, we must discover what it means to be true to ourselves. To do that we must turn to the Bible and see what it tells us about human nature and about the way our Creator made us. Then when we come to understand the proper role for sexual expression in our lives, we will be able to make more sense of sex and so recapture some of its fullness, joy, and meaning.

Genesis 1:27 teaches us that we have been made in the image of

God, that God's nature is to be our nature. If we are to know who we really are, we must acquire an accurate knowledge of who God is. Only then can we fully explore sex and its intended function in our lives.

As we examine the Bible's teachings about God, we begin to understand why secular solutions to the problems of sexuality are so insufficient. "God is Spirit" (John 4:24). Man, who was made to be in God's likeness, is therefore a combination of dust and spirit. Any solution, such as Freud's, that ignores man's spiritual nature, can lead only to emptiness and frustration. Our existential emptiness is nothing more than that uniquely God-shaped vacuum within us – a vacuum that only God's Spirit can fill. Until that void is satisfactorily occupied, we will remain frustrated. We will also be tempted to indulge the flesh in a vain effort to find the satisfaction that only God's Spirit can supply. Only God's fullness is capable of filling our inner emptiness; and as long as that void is not filled, we are easy prey to counterfeit solutions centered in personal greed and shallow sensuality.

In this vein, the Bible clearly explains why Freud's early view of love and sex led to *thanatos* (the Greed word for "death"): "If you are living according to the flesh, you must die; but if by the Spirit you are putting to death the deeds of the body, you will live. . . . For the mind set on the flesh is death, but the mind set on the Spirit is life and peace" (Rom. 8:13, 6).

In order to understand how God's Spirit enables us to be who we really are, it is important to analyze the words *image* and *likeness* as used in Genesis to describe our relationship to the Creator. The Hebrew word translated "image" is derived from the word for "shadow." It describes a representative form of an original object, and can be thought of as a concrete substance that resembles its prototype. In other words, humans were made to conform to a pattern or mold whose original is God.

People were created uniquely to be God's earthly representation. We are the divine image-bearers. The Greek word as well as the English translation for "image," is *icon*. According to 1 Corinthians 15:49, man is the earthly image of which God is the heavenly prototype. Man's very nature is like God's. Saying it another way, *what is truly natural for man is to be similar to God.*

The word *likeness* conveys a slightly different shade of meaning. With this word, the concepts of becoming and imitation are implied in the original Hebrew. Man is similar to God, but not the same. The Creator is the rule or standard we should seek to copy. God is "something toward which man was created, that he might strive after it and ultimately attain it."[2]

A person's self-image (self-concept), what he thinks of himself, has a greater impact on his behavior than perhaps any other factor. What men think of themselves decides the fate of civilization. It has been said that people were created a little lower than the angels, but recently we have preferred to think of ourselves as a little higher than the animals. Hitler's holocaust, recent atrocities in Cambodia and Afghanistan, and other examples from history indicate that humans are capable of a savagery far more vicious than that of beasts.

Genesis, then, shows us that we were made with a nature similar to God's; we were created to live in the manner of our Creator. Because we either have misunderstood what God is really like or have rejected our identification with God, we have distorted self-images. As a consequence, we often seek to live in a way that is very different from and in fact far beneath what God intended.

Most people's manner of life today is totally inconsistent with who they really are. That is why there is so much desperate emptiness; they try to fulfill their lives in ways that are contrary to their true nature. The insatiable frustration and guilt this produces is the cause of many futile wars, conflicts, and most of human suffering.

The Apostle John wrote that when Christ returns, true Christians would be like the Lord, for they would see him as he is (1 John 3:2).

The more we see what God is really like, the more we want to be like him here and now; for then we'll see that he is what we're truly like inside when at our best. Striving to be like God, therefore, is the best way to find ourselves. It's the best way to be who we're truly meant to be. It's the only way, ultimately, to be true to ourselves.

Those who try to see themselves without looking first to God will never be truly authentic. They will only imitate someone else's flawed and defective pattern for humanity. They will never find their true identity. Perhaps Augustine was right in his assertion that because God made us for himself, "Every heart is restless until it finds its rest in [him]."

WHAT IS GOD LIKE?

Since we are made in God's image, there should be a deep and familiar resonance in our soul when we understand the Bible's description of God, for it also describes what we were created to be. Scripture's premier description of the Lord is John's bold affirmation that "God is love" (1 John 4:8, 16). Love is the very essence of his nature. Doesn't this help to explain, then, why man has such an intense need for love? We need love because God is love and he created us to need him.

Yet just as Freud misunderstood man's basic needs, many people today are on the wrong trail in seeking to fulfill their deepest needs. Freud's initial belief that sex was man's primary motivating factor and greatest need was obviously mistaken. Surely sex is a powerful motivating factor, but some important historical figures lived rich and meaningful lives without giving expression to this need. Similarly, no matter how good someone's sex life is, if that person does not find genuine love, he or she can never hope to find happiness.

Several scientific studies highlight the importance of all of creation's need for love. A monkey deprived simultaneously of food and its mother will, at the point of starvation, run to its mother before seeking food. Children deprived of love grow up irreparably damaged. Some have even died.

What the New Testament calls *agape* love – the kind of love that God showed to us – is what we are to evidence in our lives. This love of God is ultimately what we need to have to be fulfilled. It is also what we must show if we are to fulfill God's purpose in our lives. Again, we need love because God created us to need him. Only as we receive his love experientially and demonstrate it can we live deeply and fully. Only then can our own need for love be satisfied. Only then can we find and be true to ourselves.

WHAT IS LOVE?

To have an accurate understanding of God and sex, we need to know not only that God is love and that we are to be like him, but also what love is like. We need a biblical definition of love. This can be confusing, because in English we use the same word to describe our affinity for peanut butter and our affection for our spouses. It's no wonder the world is so mixed up. The love that God is – that which alone is capable of satisfying our deepest needs and forever answering the question "how to be" – is very different from either sex or the eros Freud later embraced as the true solution to humanity's problem.

The love of God revealed in the New Testament is so radically different from every other love the world had known previously, that a new word had to be used to describe it. Though the Greeks had a handful of words to describe the many facets of love, none could capture the magnitude that was exposed for us in and by Jesus Christ. Perhaps it is best summed up in the oft-quoted passage in the Gospel of John: "For God so loved the world, that He gave His only begotten Son, that whosoever believes in Him should not perish, but have eternal life" (John 3:16). God loved, so he gave.

He who forbade the ancient Israelites to offer their children as sacrifices to him, as the pagans did to their gods, reserved the privilege of making such a profound sacrifice for us. He did it to prove that he would never withhold any good thing from us (Rom. 8:32). He did it to reveal the nature of the Creator to the creation he loves and desires to woo to himself. God is agape love. To know what we should be like, we must begin with this understanding of God. As he is, so are we intended to become.

People have tried to describe agape, the love that is God, in various ways. One said, very simply, that love occurs when I make your need my need. Another expanded this by saying that biblical love "means the compassionate serving of whoever stands in need, actively doing good even to one's enemies . . . and sharing one's resources with all the brethren in the Christian koinonia."[3] Love is caring more for the welfare of the beloved than for myself; since everyone is beloved by God, that means consistently putting myself last. That is quite different from our modern world's definition of love. God intends for us to live in love, not just blindly fall into it on occasion.

First Corinthians 13, known as the love chapter, is the best biblical explanation of love. It tells us what love is and isn't. Early in my Christian life I learned that I could substitute my name for the word *love* in the central verses and get a fairly accurate barometric reading on the true state of my soul. Try it yourself:

[Substitute your name for the word love] is patient,
_____ is kind, and is not jealous; _____
does not brag and is not arrogant, does not act unbecomingly;
_____ does not seek [his/her] own, _____
_____ is not provoked, does not take into account a
wrong suffered, does not rejoice in unrighteousness, but
_____ rejoices with the truth; _____
bears all things, believes all things, hopes all things, and endures all things. _____ never fails! . . ." (1 Cor.
13:4-8a)

It's obvious this kind of love isn't very natural. In fact, when
pressed to be this magnanimous, even the best of people find the
concept of sacrificial love contrary to their own instincts and fallen
human nature. This love, which I am convinced is impossible for
our natural selves to manifest, is possible only through God. So
profound and strenuous are the demands of sacrificial love that
only God himself can fulfill them.

This helps us understand why a fundamental transformation in
the very core of our being is necessary. We need love because we
are made in the image of God, who is love. We are intended to be
like him. But the law of reaping and sowing, God's justice, rules in
our world. We need love, but we are unable to sow a sufficient quantity of it that would reap enough to fill our own cavernous needs.
That's where Freud was right. Unless something changes in us
that makes it possible to give away much more love than we're born
with, we're doomed to a life of perpetual frustration.

That's where Jesus Christ comes in. He came to show us how to
live consistently with our true nature – as people made in the
image of God. He came as an incarnation of pure sacrificial love. He
then was murdered, rose from the dead, and ascended into heaven
to enable us to live as he did through his resurrected life (Rom.
8:3-4, 11, 29).

You see, the Bible repeatedly mentions this inheritance we are to
receive. (Actually it tells us that God himself is to be our inheritance in Ezekiel 44:28.) The Bible is even arranged according
to our inheritance. There's the Old Testament (a covenant, or will)
and the New. The theme of inheritance appears in Romans 8:16-17
and Hebrews 9:15, and is developed virtually throughout the entire Old and New Testaments.

Now a testament, or will, is necessary to establish the conditions for the bequest of an inheritance. The inheritance that God wished to leave us after the death of his Son is nothing less than himself. Jesus' death, resurrection, and ascension made God's Holy Spirit (John 16:7-15) available to whoever would receive him and yield their allegiance to him (John 1:12). This is the same Spirit that raised Christ from the dead (Rom. 8:11). It also empowered him to live a sinless, love-filled life (Heb. 4:15). Through his Spirit, God enabled Jesus to partake of his holiness and express his love (John 14:6-26).

Our yearning for union with our source of life, and our desire for fuller relationships, are rooted in our need for reconciliation with God. We came from him, we are intended to be like him, and nothing short of an infilling of him and his love can effectuate the transformation we truly need. We are the ones who must change – not the values of our society; society can't be made new until it has new people.

The moral values of the world don't need to be transformed to conform to humanity's carnal cravings. Every step our society takes in that direction makes the world an uglier place in which to live. The unrestrained indulgence of our selfish, fleshly instincts can never satisfy our desire for a good and noble life. Quite the contrary. It actually subjects us to darker and more deviant desires and impulses.

For people made new through an infilling of God's love, the sweetness and security of God's love makes genuine intimacy possible. Without it, they are far too insecure to be vulnerable enough to achieve authentic intimacy. It is no coincidence that monogamy came into its own in the wake of New Testament Christianity. Without an ongoing experience of God's love, it is impossible to maintain fidelity in human relationships. Apart from his coming into our lives, permanent relationships, at least those of a mutually satisfactory variety, are difficult at best. Without the Creator's involvement, procreation cannot be creative at all. In all likelihood, it will become destructive.

A world where love reigns supreme, where all live for God and consequently are committed to the betterment of one another, is the kind of world envisioned by God. This is the kind of life meant for us. But without sacrificial love, such a world is a utopian impossibility; our quest for sexual satisfaction becomes bogged down in the quicksand of irresponsible sensuality, promiscuous sex, disease, divorce, rape, abortion, homosexuality, heartbreak, and even self-destructive, violent sexual perversions. Isn't that what we're witnessing today?

With God, and only with him, we can fulfill his design for our lives. Through his love, sex can be truly life-giving and fulfilling, for he is the very essence of love. In him there is no need. Once we recognize that, we can examine his purpose behind holistically fulfilling our needs for sex, within the framework of his school of sacrifice. God is holy and therefore wholesome love. He is intent upon helping us discover the joy of being like him, and he has a specific plan for effectuating our transformation. His ways are indeed far higher than ours (Isa. 55:8-9).

EIGHT
FALSE FREEDOM

Freedom was the catchword of the sixties and early seventies. This was nowhere more true than in the area of sexuality. Explicitness became the name of the game in films, books, and language. People sought liberation from unfulfilled marriages, unplanned pregnancies, and prohibitions against premarital, extramarital, and homosexual promiscuity. Almost anywhere, we accepted the erroneous notion that real happiness would be found only by doing whatever felt good.

Eventually, even some churches became a part of this pseudo-liberation movement. Radical mainline denominational bureaucrats lobbied for unrestricted access to abortion. They championed tolerance toward divorce, premarital sex, legalized prostitution, and even homosexuality. Liberals binged on liberation of all kinds as we forgot the nature of true freedom. In all these areas, the truth of God was displaced by deceptive lies.

Ironically, pitifully, our culture's idolatrous quest for freedom led many into deeper bondage as previously undiscovered lusts became insatiable. Even some "Christians" were taken in by this New Morality. Much of this could have been avoided had they been seeking, through the lens of the Scripture, God's will for their lives so they could discern the essential differences between false freedom and the real thing.

How did this happen? Even George Orwell's secular prophetic vision, *1984*, warned us of an era of social doublespeak when men would call slavery freedom and freedom slavery. Why did we not recognize it when it happened?

Part of the churches' confusion arose because of the politicization of liberation. Around the turn of the century the social gospel movement of Christianity sought to make the church's mission germane to the concrete situations of the world. The contemporary stepchild of those concerns came to be known as liberation theology. Its defective perspective on liberation has become the philosophical undercurrent for much of the false freedom being used to perpetuate and extend the sexual revolution into the end of the twentieth century.

Liberation theology, deeply rooted in secular philosophy and Marxist social theories, arose in reaction to the escapist mentality of many religious people. It has been said that the sin of religious people reveals itself in flight from responsibility. The proponents of this theology have found fertile ground wherever Christians view their faith as relevant only to the next life and to spiritual concerns.

Christians often have failed to see the relationship between belief in God and the obligation to care for the needs of their fellowmen. Modern Christians are as guilty of separating the secular from the sacred as were our spiritual ancestors. The Israelites of old often needed the prophet's rebuke in this regard.

Liberation theology was midwifed in Latin America, due in part to the fact that many wealthy landowners, sometimes with the help of the church, oppressed the poor in their midst. In the United States, the push for civil rights by the blacks was a similar struggle against oppression. Misguided whites often twisted certain passages of Scripture to justify their racist views. It is understandable why some blacks and third world poor mistakenly came to resent the Bible.

But there are problems with liberation theology as well. First there is the assumption that freedom is an external, quantitative reality contingent upon circumstances. Landowners were thought to be free, while peasants were not. This led to prescriptions that were more Marxist than Christian: the involuntary redistribution of wealth. That in turn led to the other problems with liberation theology, its tendency to assert that the end justifies the means. If the landowners didn't like sharing their wealth, their property would just be seized. If they must be killed in the process, so be it.

True freedom, by contrast, is intrinsic—less likely to seek help materially or externally, more concerned with the quality of life. In Philippians and Acts we see that the Apostle Paul was more free than his jailers. That's why, when Christian slaves wondered how to relate to their owners, Paul's prescription was for respect rather than rebellion (cf. Eph. 6:5-9; Col. 3:22; 1 Tim. 6:1-4; and Philem.). He knew that the only revolution that could make men truly free was the regeneration that occurred within the human heart as a life became yielded to Christ's lordship (Tit. 3:3-5).

As the sexual revolution unfolded, feminists and homosexuals cloaked their radical, immoral agendas in the respectable garb of civil rights, enabling them to win support from some religious institutions. They took the warped biblical treatments of the liberation theologians and applied them to areas of gender and sexual preference. They sought to make the causes of feminists and homosexuals appear to be civil rights issues where the minority was "oppressed" by the majority's social concensus. Both groups saw society's sexual mores and taboos as a bondage forced upon them from an outside source. Each believed that evil was systemic, rooted in "corrupt" social and religious institutions and values. Each thought the Bible was an anachronism that was being unrighteously used against them. As a result, they labored to change the social systems and standards they considered ignorant and outdated, in an attempt to establish "social justice" for women and homosexuals and cast their agendas into the malleable political arena as well.

Liberation theology, rooted in a misinterpretation of biblical teaching, twists and perverts the Scriptures to arrive at what seems to be a biblical ideology. The coercive, sometimes violent political methods used to implement these ideals are thoroughly ungodly. Their attempts to extend the kingdom of God have been little more than self-righteous acts which usually only further complicate the problems of the groups they have sought to help. Much that is done today in its name on the home and foreign mission fields is diametrically opposed to the purposes of God. This is true whether addressing the advocacy of guerrilla violence in Latin America and Africa, or the use of United Methodist facilities and offerings to support radical pro-abortion, feminist, and homosexual agendas. Those who do this work and those who knowingly support them are so blinded by their attempts to establish their own righteousness that they can't see the harm they are doing.

This is true in regard to both third-world missions, which aid and abet the violent work of so-called "people's liberation" guerrilla groups, or the hate-filled, bigoted writings of black theologians which fueled the race riots that rocked our country in the sixties. It is equally true of feminist authors whose works have led unwittingly to a diminished quality of life for many women, and of American university ministries that encourage a student to accept his or her alleged homosexual orientation rather than find Christ's power to repent.

The Lord does indeed care about the poor and those who are oppressed and in bondage. He has promised to liberate the captives. But if we are to understand how the Lord would extend his kingdom's reign and deal righteously with injustice, we need his perspective on the source of human oppression. We must also learn about his ways of bringing authentic liberation to persons. To be genuine agents of God's liberating righteousness, we must adopt biblical methods for achieving godly ends. Primitive Christianity changed the world as nothing else in history could. We can see similar results in our generation: the things Jesus did and greater things we can do (John 14:12). However, if we would see New Testament results we must use New Testament methods. The righteous end cannot seduce us into using corrupt means to achieve it.

The Scripture passage most people use as an ideological foundation for a theology of liberation is Jesus' inaugural statement. It is a text that established the tone and thrust for all of his teachings and earthly ministry. It is a passage he quotes from Isaiah 61, recorded in Luke 4:18-19 (AMP.):

> The Spirit of the Lord is upon Me, because He has anointed Me . . . to preach the good news . . . to the poor; . . . announce release to the captives, and recovery of sight to the blind; to send forth delivered those who are oppressed—who are downtrodden, bruised, crushed and broken down by calamity; to proclaim the . . . acceptable year of the Lord—the day when salvation and the free favors of God profusely abound.

What is the Good News that Jesus preached to the poor? Was it that Rome must provide for them a minimum standard of living? How did he release the captives? Was it through revolutionary

80

overthrow of the Roman rule? How did he deliver the slaves who were downtrodden, crushed, and oppressed? Was it by transposing them into a position of financial equality with their oppressor?

Of course Jesus' message of liberation, the Good News he came to bring us, was different from all of this.

> Jesus attached great importance to the conversion of the individual. He led no protest march to Rome or Jerusalem advocating social reform. The social injustices of the day must have caused him anguish. The poverty and misery of the masses contrasted with the revels of the wealthy, the sickness and disease, the tax-ridden tenant farmers, the blatant injustice on every hand—the heavy yoke of Rome—all this must have been a source of deepest personal sorrow for him. Yet he resisted the temptation to make a dramatic demand for social justice. He did not command his followers to concern themselves primarily with these obvious evils.[1]

It was Judas Iscariot (the betrayer of Christ) who was unrealistically obsessed with giving to the impoverished (Matt. 26:6-16). The true disciples offered no silver or gold, but rather were concerned with healing the very root problem that caused a person to depend on others (Acts 3:3-8). Similarly Jesus rejected all attempts to set himself up as a ruler of this world (John 18:36). He repeatedly stated that his kingdom was not of this world and men could not use carnal means to extend its authority (Matt. 26:50-56).

Rather than dealing with the superficial symptoms that seemed to most people to be the problems of his age, Jesus penetrated to the heart of men's problems. He taught that people were really oppressed from within themselves—by sin (Mark 7:14-23). This is what keeps them from finding the wholeness, self-actualization, and true freedom that he came to bring (Matt. 5:6).

Jesus came to set us free, not to do what we want, but to do what we ought; not to do our thing, but to do God's. He knew that only those who were capable of doing God's will would be able to experience real freedom: "If you abide in My word, then you are truly disciples of Mine; and you shall know the truth, and the truth shall make you free. . . . Truly, truly I say to you, everyone who commits sin is the slave of sin. And the slave does not remain in the house forever; the son does remain forever. If therefore the Son shall make you free, you shall be free indeed" (John 8:31-36).

It is not others' hatred and rejection that destroys us, but our response to that hatred and rejection. That response decides whether we will be liberated so as to experience the joy of Christ, who triumphed over the unjust evil of men, or be enslaved from within by the hatred and resentment lodged in our own hearts. For that reason, Jesus took away our sins (Matt. 1:21). And his theology of liberation works. Paul wrote more exuberantly about the joy of the Lord while in the most abject prision situations. (Joy is one of Paul's dominant subjects throughout Philippians.)

This is the message of true liberation that needs to be heard by men and women today. Jesus Christ can liberate us from the prison of our own sins, false pride, inner bitterness, and resentment. Those who fail to perceive that this is the real meaning of the gospel have yet to see the kingdom. "There is a way that seems right to a man" and most people, lacking spiritual insight (John 3:3), are hell-bent on following it. It is the way that leads not to life and wholeness but to death and destruction (Prov. 14:12). The truths that the Bible teaches, though directly contrary to our natural inclinations (Rom. 8:5-14), were written to help us find peace and fulfillment. They are the very words of life.

Those who seek to define freedom as the world does, the right to do whatever is natural and feels good, lead people into a deeper and more serious form of bondage. No one in our age has described this deception better than Kahlil Gibran. In *The Prophet*, he wrote:

> I have seen the freest among you wear their freedom as a yoke and a handcuff. And my heart bled within me; for you can only be free when even the desire of seeking freedom becomes a harness to you, and when you cease to speak of freedom as a goal and a fulfillment. . . . And how shall you rise beyond your days and nights unless you break the chains which you at the dawn of your understanding have fastened around your noon hour? In truth that which you call freedom is the strongest of these chains, though its links glitter in the sun and dazzle your eyes.[2]

Those so blinded by their own need for freedom have done all they could to destroy the social institutions they consider responsible for the enslavement of people. Typical of their misguided efforts is this statement from a major feminist document:

> The end of the institution of marriage is a necessary condition for the liberation of women. Therefore it is important for us to encourage women to leave their husbands and not to live individually with men. . . . [Marriage] has failed us and we must work to destroy it. . . . [3]

Such people have not, however, been satisfied with the destruction of institutions. They have gone to the very soul of life to exorcise from individuals the thing they consider to be the true source of suffering and enslavement:

> We must destroy love. . . . Love promotes vulnerability, dependence, possessiveness, susceptibility to pain, and prevents the full development of woman's human potential by directing all her energies outward in the interest of others. [4]

Though the attempt to destroy love is doomed to failure, it nevertheless has succeeded, unfortunately, in snuffing out love in the hearts of many who have become embittered by their own frustrated hopes, desires, and needs. The church should be an agent of inner healing and deliverance for these people as well as a bulwark of truth against the half-truths that have enslaved them.

It should become increasingly evident to those who have eyes to see it, that he who invented sex also seeks to teach us to possess this great gift instead of allowing it to possess us. Sexual sin leads to enslavement, not freedom. Understanding that is the secret, not only of finding true freedom, but also of receiving other precious treasures that he has in store for those who love him (1 Cor. 2:9).

NINE
THE MARVELOUS
ONE-FLESH MYSTERY

Biblically, the only context in which sexual intercourse is condoned is within the sanctuary of marriage between a man and a woman. Until recent years, the wisdom of this position was generally accepted by our society. But since the sexual revolution of the sixties, premarital sex (fornication), adultery, and homosexuality have been increasingly accepted by secular society and even by certain liberal segments of Christendom.

When Jesus said a man should leave his parents and cleave to his wife to become one flesh (Matt. 19:5), he referred to something far more profound than their physical coupling. The Apostle Paul describes their mystical union as a sublime mystery; one that reveals significant things about the relationship between Jesus, our eternal Bridegroom, and his bride, the Church (Eph. 5:31-32).

Couples who fail to comprehend the essence of the marvelous one-flesh mystery will probably be unable to fully appreciate the richness of their own sexual experience. Unless they understand and cooperate with the heavenly Husband's plan for the marriage relationship, the soul satisfaction so essential to their inner well-being will elude them. The sexual communion that our Lord intended to be a perpetually growing, deepening, and enriching experience can easily degenerate into a shriveling, embittering, and destructive encounter. When that happens, a marriage intended to be an oasis of love and support for a couple is soon swallowed up by life's bewildering deserts. Without God's help the most promising of marriages can become "a duel in the midst of a war."

MARRIAGE: A MICROCOSM OF GOD'S LOVE

Because a Christian marriage is in microcosm God's relationship to his people, permanence and fidelity are essential to its success. I didn't always believe that permanence was important. Having been raised in a liberal Protestant church, I thought the Roman Catholic prohibition against divorce was archaic and inhumane. I was sure that a loving God would not require people to be trapped in a "bad marriage." Imagine my surprise, around the time of my conversion, when I stumbled across Matthew 5:31-32: "And it was said, 'Whoever sends his wife away, let him give her a certificate of divorce'; but I say to you that everyone who divorces his wife, except for the cause of unchastity, makes her commit adultery; and whoever marries a divorced woman commits adultery."

In a similar passage in Matthew 19:4-6, Jesus links this mandate to the unifying function of marriage. If two people become one, tearing them apart would cause them both irreparable damage. The disciples found this to be a hard statement, one that would make marriage a thing to be forsaken. I was prone to agree, until I knew God better.

As mentioned previously, marriage is designed primarily to crucify our selfishness and fashion within us the true nature of God. Marriage can teach us to love sacrificially and shape us for fulfilling God's purposes in our lives. When the Lord speaks of two people becoming one flesh, he alludes to that transformation. The word *flesh* does not just refer to our physical bodies. It's a term used to designate the "dynamic principle of sinfulness."[1] It describes our carnal desires and willfulness, our "self-wrought corruption." Those who live after the flesh, pursuing totally selfish goals, are incapable of following the ways of the Spirit (Rom. 8:6-8). No one can go east and west at the same time. Those who try tear themselves apart.

Marriage is uniquely designed to devastate this innate, self-defeating human tendency. For two people to become one flesh (one in purpose, will, and desire), they must each subordinate their needs and desires to the highest good for their mate. That's why fifty-fifty marriages do not work. Only the marriage in which both partners give 100 percent can thrive. The extent to which a person learns to live for the well-being of his or her mate largely determines the extent to which their married life will reflect the glory of

God who sent his Son to teach us the secret of life: that it is more blessed to give than receive (Acts 20:35).

THE BIBLICAL CONCEPT OF COVENANT

To comprehend marriage and the reason for its importance as a biblical symbol reflecting the purposes of God, we must understand the biblical concept of covenant. Covenant is the unifying and organizing principle of the entire Bible. The Bible is divided into two parts on the basis of the Old and New Covenants (Testaments). Covenant is the key relationship that enables God to fulfill his purposes with humankind and creation. It is also the key to accomplishing his purposes in and through a marriage.

A covenant is a binding agreement between two parties. In the Bible it is intended to eternally yoke people together with God and one another for their mutual and highest good. Biblical covenants are effectuated by death and maintained by sacrifice (Exod. 24:8; Heb. 9:16-20).

That's essentially why Jesus had to die. He had a body of flesh just like ours. He also had a will of his own. Though he was God in the flesh, he had the very real possibility of going his own way; of resisting the purposes of God. He had to choose to lay down his life for us. No one could take it from him (John 10:17-18). He also had the freedom to choose *not* to be the sacrifice we required.

Because Jesus chose to die for us, certain benefits became ours. If we think of the Lord's covenant with us as a will or testament, we realize that until Jesus died we couldn't receive what he wanted to give us. As long as a person is alive, the heirs cannot use what is bequeathed to them.

Historically, Christians have recognized that Jesus' sacrificial death purchased eternal life for us. This is the very essence of our inheritance as sons and daughters of God. We must realize, however, that the benefits of eternal life begin to accrue to our account in this life in the form of temporal blessings. Jesus died to give us these blessings. The best news is that his resurrection enables him through the Holy Spirit to help us know how to wisely invest and enjoy our inheritance. The spiritual ecstasies that the indwelling Holy Spirit shares with us in our communion with God find their only earthly parallel in the ecstasies of sexual intercourse. But the benefits don't stop there. A primary purpose for our heavenly Father's discipline of us is designed "for our profit, that we might be partakers of his holiness" (Heb. 12:10, KJV). It is, after all, the *Holy* Spirit that we've received.

The Holy Spirit is given to us to help make us like God. Since God is holy (Isa. 6:3 and elsewhere) and we are made in his image, the Holy Spirit is given to enable us to live consistently as we really are designed to do, and thus fulfill our true and highest purpose.

In a real sense, then, because the Holy Spirit is a spirit, he can fulfill our inner needs. Because he is holy, he can enable us to translate God's indwelling presence into our external behavior. This empowers us to live as fully and obediently as God intended. As our walk in the Holy Spirit progresses with Jesus, the eternal Bridegroom, we learn to know God better. The better we know him as he truly is, and witness his love for us as revealed in his unfolding plan for our lives, the more we desire to fulfill his will for us. As we do this, imperfections are worked out of us and our lives become truly whole.

Jesus' death for us, however, does far more for us than release our eternal inheritance. Because he spared not his own life for us, we can live for him. We can trust that he cares for our well-being more than his own. This is the real message of the one-flesh mystery. God is *for* us (Rom. 8:31)! He intensely cares about showing us how to live blessed lives.

UNDERSTANDING THE ONE-FLESH MYSTERY

I first came to understand the essence of the one-flesh mystery when I was seeking the Lord's will about getting married.

One major reason for my coming to the Lord was dissatisfaction with being single and running around with a lot of women. Part of the bait used by the Master Fisher of men to draw me into his net was the hope and promise of a simple, loving family life based on a faithful marriage to a kind, godly woman. That was in 1971. By 1976 I was still single, and my search for the right person had led me through many wrong and frustrating experiences.

I had blundered through all the phases that many single Christians put themselves through and probably some no one else has ever experienced. Three different women told me that the Lord wanted me to marry them. Two other times I was equally certain I'd found *the* person God had for me, only to be proven wrong and end up heartbroken. I then thought that I had to be a "bachelor till the rapture" in order to serve God fully, until I became equally persuaded that unless I married and my needs for love and sex were met, I could not even keep my Christian life together.

Finally, after becoming thoroughly discouraged with this exasperating emotional roller coaster, I decided to seek the Lord every day until I knew whether he wanted me to marry or stay single, and if he wanted me to marry, who I was to wed and when.

I'd never sought the Lord like this before and hardly knew how to begin. I discovered, though, that in so doing I was embarking on an exhilarating and enlightening journey, one that did more to increase my knowledge of God than a year in seminary ever could.

Six weeks from the day when I vowed to seek the Lord daily to resolve my question about marriage, I met my wife-to-be. Then things really began popping. I proposed on our first date. Two weeks later she accepted, and less than four months after that we were married.

There are many amazing things I learned about our heavenly Father in those six weeks. Space does not permit me to share all of them with you, but the most remarkable thing, something that has eternally improved my walk with God, has to do with the one-flesh mystery.

For years I had wondered what the core mystery was that Paul had alluded to in Ephesians 5:28-33. He compared a godly marriage to Jesus' relationship with the Church. In describing the husband's role, which I am convinced is at least as profoundly difficult as the wife's, he said:

> So husbands ought also to love their own wives as their own bodies. He who loves his own wife loves himself; for no one ever hated his own flesh, but nourishes and cherishes it, just as Christ also does the church, because we are members of His body. FOR THIS CAUSE A MAN SHALL LEAVE HIS FATHER AND MOTHER, AND SHALL CLEAVE TO HIS WIFE; AND THE TWO SHALL BECOME ONE FLESH. This mystery is great; but I am speaking with reference to Christ and the church. Nevertheless let each in-

dividual among you also love his own wife even as himself;
and let the wife see to it that she respect her husband.

For years I'd pondered that passage and learned many valuable
things from it, but I was haunted by the belief that there was something crucial in it that I'd never really comprehended. I knew that
in this passage was something significant I needed to know about
God and his relationship with me that was veiled from my eyes –
something that should be reflected in a Christian marriage.

During my six-week quest to discern the Lord's purposes for me,
I kept turning back to Ephesians 5. I would read and reread this
passage, but somehow I could never quite grasp it. By this time,
the Lord had shown me that he wanted me to marry (Prov. 18:22;
1 Cor. 7:2; Eccles. 9:9), and that he would soon bring someone new
into my life for that reason. I had yet to meet her, though, and I
sensed that the Lord first had things to teach me about him and
about myself.

On the particular day he opened my eyes to the one-flesh mystery, I was struggling with whether I wanted to be married. Have
you ever experienced how the Lord brings us to a neutral place
concerning our heart's desire by showing us the price we must pay
to make our dreams come true? Because of my friendship with a
young Christian woman, I was reflecting on the negative aspects of
marriage. I was thinking how often it was hard for men to understand women, and realizing that marriage would require me to
relinquish a great deal of personal liberty. Most important, though,
I was thinking about how vulnerable love would make me. I was
remembering the agonizing heartbreak of past relationships that
had soured.

I knew that even when Christian relationships hold people together, they often exact a painful price. I knew that the Lord asks
men to love their wives as Christ loves the Church. I remembered
that his love for us had required Jesus to lay down his life for us. I
translated that into the multitudinous sacrifices, the daily dying to
self, that I knew would be required in a Christian marriage.

As I reflected on this anticipated self-denial, I sensed that the
Lord was asking me if I would lay down my life for the woman he
wanted to give me. Deep within, memories of hurt, rejection, and
humiliating failure in past relationships cascaded upon me, and I
found myself saying, "Lord, I can't die to myself for a woman. It will

hurt too much." From deep inside, his still small voice said so reassuringly and lovingly, "But I can."

I suddenly realized that Jesus' suffering and rejection, his humiliation and death on the cross, were for just such a time as this in my life. He took my griefs, sorrows, and pains upon himself (Isa. 53:4-6), so that when I needed to suffer and die to myself I could draw on his resources to accomplish what otherwise would have been humanly impossible. Something inside of me broke. I said, "OK, Lord. If you'll do it through me I will. . . . I'll lay down my life for the woman you want to give me. I will give myself to loving her as you love me."

Immediately I was filled with peace. My inner turmoil was over. The battle of my will was won once again for the side of God's best.

I felt an urging to rush back to my apartment and reread Ephesians 5. Finally, the familiar words made sense. As is so often the case, I had to be willing to do God's will in order to more fully understand it (John 7:17). "No one ever hated his own flesh, but nourishes and cherishes it, just as Christ also does the church, because we are members of His body" (Eph. 5:29-30). Since Jesus had already taken upon himself the pain of my own death to myself, I was open to receive an entirely new insight about God: Because I am a part of his body, he is no more interested in harming me than I am in shooting myself in the foot.

Through the Holy Spirit, who became available to me as I yielded my will to God (John 1:12-13), I became one with Christ. Because I am one with him in purpose, I am joined to him in spirit: I become organically united to the God who is spirit. His pain becomes mine and mine his. That means he nourishes and cherishes me and only wants for me what will truly be for my highest good. This releases me to seek to honor and obey him in everything since he will never ordain for me anything that is not in my best interest.

Before I entered into this six-week search to know the specific will of God, I had a warped perspective of God. This was revealed to me in my devotional life one day. During my prayer time I had been begging and pleading with the Lord to heed my request for a wife. I then opened a book I'd been using for devotions. It said:

> None ever sought me in vain. I wait, wait with a hungry longing to be called upon; and I, who have already seen your heart's needs before you cried upon Me, before perhaps you

were conscious of those needs yourself, I am already preparing the answer.

It is like a mother, who is setting aside suitable gifts for her daughter's wedding, before Love even has come into the daughter's life.

The *Anticipatory Love* of God is a thing mortals seldom realize. Dwell on this thought. Dimiss from your minds the thought of a grudging God, who had to be petitioned with sighs and tears and much speaking before reluctantly He loosed the desired treasures. Man's thoughts of Me need revolutionizing.

Try and see a mother preparing birthday or Christmas delights for her child–the while her mother-heart sings: "Will she not love that? How she will love this!" and anticipates the rapture of her child, her own heart full of the tenderest joy? From Me–a faint echo this of My preparation–joy.

Try to see this as plans unfold of my preparing. It means much to Me to be understood, and the understanding of Me will bring great joy to you.[2]

I read this January 19, 1976. This insight into the heart of God forever transformed my theology. He who had seemed so stingy and grudging suddenly appeared to me as he really is: a kind and generous Father who delights in providing his children with their hearts' desires (Ps. 37:4; 1 Tim. 6:17b). On January 31 I met my wife-to-be. On February 14 we were engaged.

Why do I share this with you? Because it is intimately related to a proper understanding and knowledge of God; a knowledge that is essential to the development of a healthy marriage. And that kind of marriage is paramount to a fully rewarding sex life. Sex is far more complex and wonderful than just a great indoor sport.

I needed to realize that Jesus' death on the cross was a sacrifice he willingly made for me, because he loved me. Beyond that, I needed to know that his love was not just a "this hurts-me-more-than-it-hurts-you" type of disciplinary love. I needed to know that the Lord delights in blessing me. I needed to discover that my groveling attempts at manipulating God into heeding my requests were thoroughly unnecessary. Because I am one with him, he is as interested in my happiness as he is in his own. The two are inextricably interrelated. Until I knew that, I was unable to trust the Lord with my needs and desires and consequently yield to him my heartfelt obedience. Furthermore, I couldn't delight in his love for me.

Another element compounded my ability to trust God. I was painfully aware of my shortcomings. Earlier in my Christian life the Lord showed me that even though I had received his Holy Spirit and sought to enthrone Jesus as Lord of my life, I was still capable of desperately depraved acts. I had become almost hopelessly enmeshed in some serious sins. (All sins are serious, some just seem to be more so.) He had persuaded me, through that period, of his unabated love – he would never leave nor forsake me (Heb. 13:5) – and that had pulled me through. As I received his grace I became newly liberated from my bondage to the sins of my past, but I was still poignantly aware of my own frailty. How could a mighty and holy God ever be pleased with a feeble and sin-stained creature such as me?

This experience of having him look beyond my past and present weakness reminded me anew of the eternal quality of his love. He knows how weak we are. He made us this way; but, like a father pities his immature, disobedient children, so the Lord took compassion on me (Ps. 103:13-18).

All of these experiences with God's love had an exuberatingly liberating effect on my own soul and served to prepare me for my new role as a Christian husband. *Once we comprehend that someone knows us at our worst and refuses to turn away in disgust, we know we can trust and yield to their love.*

As surely as a person needs to know these things about God's love, just as certainly he needs to reflect these same qualities to his spouse. The degree of emotional intimacy that a man and woman attain and the quality of their love for one another affects the extent of their mutual sexual satisfaction.

INTERPERSONAL KNOWLEDGE

This whole matter of interpersonal knowledge is a crucial and recurrent biblical theme. Jesus said of certain religious people who did wonderful deeds in his name that their lives were in vain and their deeds evil. The reason? He never knew them (Matt. 7:20-23).

This is an amazing statement. Who is there that Jesus doesn't know? I believe he really was saying their relationship with him was so insecure that they would not allow him to expose their evil hearts. They were unwilling to see that their religious activity was self-serving and pretentious, designed to disguise the evil within themselves that they were unwilling to honestly face and deal with. Thus they hid themselves from a true knowledge of God and sought, by their religious activity, to earn what can never be bought: the freely given favor and unconditional acceptance of God.

The Lord uses the verb *to know* to denote the most intimate form of sexual communion between a man and his wife—Adam knew his wife and she begat (Gen. 4:1). The implications are clear. Sexual relations and intimacy that are based on an authentic knowledge of your mate are fruitful and pleasing to God. *Conversely, genuine intimacy is impossible for pretentious people.* They can only relate to a mirage. Without such intimacy, the sex act quickly degenerates into a relatively empty, boring, and meaningless physical exercise. Such an experience can never offer true satisfaction.

Just as God's covenant with us enables us to be inextricably joined to him for mutual benefit, so also does a permanent marriage covenant work for the mutual well-being of a Christian couple. As Bonhoeffer once said, prior to the wedding a couple's love holds their relationship together. Afterward their commitment to one another preserves their love.

When people are eternally yoked together, their love will endure the hard times. Beyond that, however, and of far greater significance is the fact that they will never have to ask one another, "Will you still love me tomorrow?" Such security fosters an environment in which true intimacy is possible. It enables a man and woman to be themselves and to love each other vulnerably. In such an environment, emotional and interpersonal maturity can develop. In such a marriage the sex act can become a growing, nurturing expression of one's care for the well-being of one's mate.

Certainly not all marriages achieve this harmony or even aspire to this level of growth. Too few people are even aware of the opportunities their marriages provide for such maturation and intimacy. No temporary relationship can ever provide for or sustain this kind of interpersonal growth. That's why adultery and fornication can never do for a person what marriage can. Homosexual relationships have their own unique deficiencies, which are discussed in a later chapter.

We have only scratched the surface of the many valuable and enduring dynamics at work in a godly marriage. Such a relationship is a treasury of insights into the very heart of the eternal love of God and his ways with men. The mystery of his desire to be one with us is the secret to understanding the rest – his covenant with us is the paradoxically binding key that unlocks our hearts to receive his blessings. No wonder the purposes of God are incomprehensible to an unspiritual person (1 Cor. 2:12-16).

Because God has chosen to be one with any who receive him and yield their will to him, he has, in his person, given us a clear vision for a successful marriage. As he has identified his well-being and the success of his purposes with us, so ought husband and wife do the same with one another. They are no longer to function independently, but in harmony with each other's deepest needs and desires. When a wife submits the control of her life to her husband and he accepts responsibility for her highest good, their lives become inextricably intertwined, their well-being avoidably interrelated. For one to hurt the other is to harm him or herself.

With God's help they can trust one another deeply. More significantly, they can become faithful stewards of this trust. Then they will be much happier together than they ever could have been apart, and the most painful part of their adjustment to one another will be over. No longer need they fight for their own way. Instead they can seek together to know and experience God's best. Their wills become one through union with God's. That union alone can produce the peace, well-being, and love that each desires.

TEN
THE SCHOOL OF SACRIFICE

Some years ago, pop psychologists prophesied the demise of marriage as an institution. In recent years, however, marriage has made a remarkable recovery. Even traditional ceremonies are "in" again and the divorce rate is tapering off. The reason for this is reflected perhaps in a 1976 *Redbook* survey.[1] Eight out of ten people polled felt that a deeply satisfying intimate relationship with another person is the most important ingredient in a happy life. Such a relationship far outranked all other options including sex, money, power, beauty, and prestige.

Marriage, properly designed, is still the best vehicle for achieving the goal of personal intimacy. Even the authors of a book advocating "open marriage" have recanted, acknowledging the failure of their marriage-without-monogamy theories.

Few couples, however, have discovered how to make their marriages live up to their hopes and dreams. Adultery, homosexuality, and domestic violence are increasing even among Christians who would never condone such enigmatic behavior.

Why is marriage such a difficult experience for so many? How can people fashion their marriages to fulfill their own high expectations? Perhaps more relevant to the subject of this book is the question of how sex within the confines of marriage can become a continually growing and satisfying experience. Must monogamy lead to monotony?

THE PURPOSE OF MARRIAGE

The premise of this chapter is that few people understand the real purpose of marriage. Fewer still understand how it relates to their total needs as people made in the image of God. Too often, sex and marriage have been examined as separate entities, apart from the totality of man's nature and a fuller understanding of his purpose in life.

Unfortunately, even clergy have done little to clarify the purpose of marriage. Few pastors require extensive premartial counseling today. When they do they usually limit their discussion to sex, roles, communication, in-laws, and finances. All these things are important, to be sure, but unless both husband and wife have an adequate grasp of the real purpose of marriage, they will probably stumble blindly through a lot of unnecessary problems. They will be ill-equipped to interpret and manage marriage's inevitable struggles and conflicts redemptively. In fact, their union may not even survive, let alone thrive.

Most young couples enter into marriage for the purpose of meeting their needs. Marriage can in fact meet their needs, but usually not as they hope. Marriage does not automatically fill a person's emptiness with a blissful overflow of emotional fulfillment and sexual satisfaction. Rather, marriage is designed to teach people how to genuinely love. For that reason, many of its lessons are more painful than passionate. And yet, as we shall see, this is exactly what we need. Once a person begins to learn how to genuinely love his mate and others, the most profound needs of his life can be authentically fulfilled.

The Bible says much to us about marriage; in fact marriage is one of Scripture's key themes. The Bible initiates the story of humankind with a discussion of our sexual differences (Gen. 1:27) and culminates history with a description of the wedding feast of God's Son and his eternal bride, the Church. Between Genesis and Revelation, the Bible is packed with indications of the profound importance of marriage in God's scheme of things. The marriage metaphor is used more than any other as a synonym for God and is synonymous with the word *husband* (1 Peter 3:6 and elsewhere).

Whole books of the Bible (Song of Solomon, Hosea, and sections of others) are devoted to the marriage metaphor and to the problems of spiritual and physical infidelity. The very word used to describe adultery *(unfaithfulness)* is the opposite of the word used to commend the obedient *(faithful)*. Marriage customs in Bible times are described in detail and teach us much about God's ways with man. They play an essential part in the rich symbolism of Jesus' parables (Matt. 25:1-12; Mark 2:19-20; and others). The Apostle Paul goes so far as to say the biblical marriage relationship between a husband and wife reveals much to us concerning the relationship between Christ and his bride (Eph. 5:21-33). This is probably what German theologian Karl Barth meant when he called marriage a paradigm (pattern) of the kingdom of God.

THE SOLUTION FOR SELFISHNESS

What's so significant about marriage? Why is this symbol so important to God? What does marriage reveal to us about God's relationship with us and the Lord's provision for our deepest needs?

Perhaps these questions can best be answered in light of the Russian philosopher Berdyaev's description of marriage. He calls it the "school of sacrifice." As such its curriculum is one that few of us would willingly choose as an elective. This may explain the wisdom behind the blissfully blinding experience of romantic love. Many who view the struggles of marriage realistically allow those struggles to obscure its blessings. Some avoid marriage like the plague.

We might well wonder why anyone would choose to learn the strenuous lessons that sacrifice teaches us. In fact, the spiritually insensitive person may never understand (1 Cor. 2:10-16). The cross upon which selfishness is mortally wounded seems foolish to those whose inner eyes have never beheld eternity (1 Cor. 1:18). To one who has tasted the goodness of the age to come and has partaken of the wonderful love of God, the wisdom that sacrificial living imparts is no longer distasteful.

Remember, we were made to be like God, and he is sacrificial love. Being true to who we were created to be means living a life of sacrificial love.

Paradoxically, when we obsessively try to fill the inner void with our own selfish pursuits, we find frustration, not fulfillment. Everything in the kingdom of God is upside down. In reality, selfishness is ultimately counterproductive. This is the meaning behind Jesus' statement that he who tries to save his life shall lose it (Matt. 19:29). If, on the other hand, we comprehend that it is certainly more blessed to give than to receive (Acts 20:35), we are on our way to discovering the real secret to personal satisfaction: "Whoever loses his life for My sake shall find it" (Matt. 16:25).

The real life Jesus refers to begins in this life and goes on into the next. The essence of eternal life is loving sacrificially. "Everyone who loves is born of God and knows God. He who does not love does not know God" (1 John 4:7-8, NKJV). As Henry Drummond said so poignantly, life is not a playground; rather it's a school in which the greatest lesson to be learned is the lesson of love.[2] As we learn to love, we live in increasingly closer union with the God who is love (1 John 4:16). This essentially guarantees that our inner needs will be legitimately met. In turn, we become insulated from the ravages of unrestrained sensual indulgence. The person who has feasted wouldn't consider eating from a garbage can. When you have Perrier, why drink from a sewer?

The benefits of learning to love don't stop there, however. Since justice ultimately rules the universe and superintends the affairs of men, we do reap what we sow. The one who spends a life planting seeds of love will reap a rich harvest of loving relationships and interpersonal success and happiness. When we are so loved, we have few other needs.

That is precisely why marriage is so important. It is uniquely designed to accelerate our capacity for learning to love. It is impossible to live in intimate proximity to another human being of the opposite sex and not be tutored by the schoolmarm of sacrifice. Those who joyfully embrace this higher form of education will discover the real purpose of marriage. It is remarkably well equipped to train us in the ways of sacrificial love and thus make us more godly. The ones to whom this will not be good news are those who don't know they have been made to be like Christ, or whose view of God has been sufficiently warped to prevent them from seeing him as he really is.

The person who sees God as he truly is will desire to be like him. Our identification with our Creator and our capacity to reflect his glorious life to our love-starved world is the essence of authentic self-actualization. Those who give themselves to these goals will expand their own individual potential far beyond the bounds of mere human possibilities as they learn the delectable secret of living out of the divine Source.

100

THE ROLE OF SEX

We do well to wonder what role sex plays in effecting the life-transforming processes of a healthy marriage relationship. If we limit our appreciation of sex to its procreational purposes, we miss some significant contributions sex makes to the Lord's goal of making us more loving and more lovely people.

Sex, first of all, entices us to enter into the marriage relationship. It's not the only reason why people get married, but it is certainly a strong inducement. A good friend who has been a pastor for almost fifty years once told me, "God knew if he didn't make marriage compellingly appealing, very few of us would pay its exorbitant price tag." In this sense, sex is especially paradigmatic of our relationship with God. Most people initially come to God out of their overwhelming needs. As anyone who has had his heart flooded with the love of God can testify, one cannot experience the bliss of his Spirit's presence and not desire more.

As the promise of love and sex lures us into marriage, the delicious nectar of God's love lures us into a deeper relationship with him. The renewing presence of God's Spirit, especially sweet and available when life on the straight and narrow becomes most strenuous, enables us to honor our commitment to God.

Sex serves a similar function in a permanently committed marriage, but it does other things to make us more Christlike as well. As tithing is a tangible symbolic expression of our commitment to God of all we have, so also is sex a significant symbol of a person's marriage commitment to his or her mate. In a Christian marriage, a husband and a wife are to be perpetually available to each other sexually (1 Cor. 7:3-5). In a person's relationship to God we are not our own; we were bought with a price and we belong to God (1 Cor. 6:19-20). The same is true in a couple's relationship to one another. They are no longer their own. Rather, they belong to each other. To withhold themselves from each other sexually, except by mutual agreement for short periods of prayer and fasting, is fraudulent (1 Cor. 7:5). Fraud is defined as an "intentional deception to cause a person to give up property or some lawful right." The fraudulent person is an "imposter" and "cheat"; one "who is not what he pretends to be."[3] In this case the property that is not yours, but another's, is your own body. In a Christian marriage, your body belongs to your mate.

Lovingly giving up your sexual rights to your mate is but a small physical expression of a more significant reality in the truly Christian marriage. That reality is that the husband and wife no longer live for themselves alone. God's goal in their relationship is to effectuate a spiritual and volitional union between the two people making them literally one with each other. Their physical coupling is but a foretaste of that union, their sexual availability a means for effectuating it.

Few things knit a couple together more effectively than the knowledge that they are physically and emotionally "there for one another." Few have greater potential for alienation than the knowledge that your mate is not truly yours. In this sense, sex becomes a testing ground for the marriage commitment. It becomes an important vehicle for helping the husband and wife flesh out their commitment to selflessly serve one another. Each time they pass this test another nail is driven more deeply into the old selfish nature, another opportunity embraced for experiencing the joy of sacrificial love.

The couple's obedience to the commandment to be sexually available also strengthens their relationship with God. Because the marriage partners' capacity to enjoy sex is intricately related to the current quality of their relationship to each other, they must be careful to be aware of the dynamics at work in all facets of their relationship. This teaches them the sensitivity of Christ. Each time a person is faced with a request from his or her mate, an opportunity is afforded to tap anew into the Spirit of Christ, to ask for the wisdom and the wherewithal to respond with love.

Jesus never indulged his body's desire to avoid the pain of sacrificial commitment. Through his indwelling Spirit, Christ's strength is available to us to overrule our human weakness; his generosity to supplant our selfishness. Those who learn to subordinate their desires and call on Christ for help will learn something very important to their entire life: God's supply is greater than their need. That which is impossible for humans, the laying down of their own needs, wants, and desires, is God-possible (Matt. 19:26). That which they find difficult is easy for the Spirit within.

The implications of these lessons extend far beyond the marriage relationship. When we are available to honor the commitment that Christ's love has led us to make, his power and life in the Holy Spirit are available to enable us to honor those commitments. But in the flesh, under the influences of our own carnal human nature, it is impossible to live and love sacrificially. That's what makes a biblical life-style so repugnant to people devoid of his Spirit. Not only does obedience run contrary to their carnal nature, but it is actually impossible for unredeemed people to fully obey God.

In his death and resurrection (2 Cor. 5:14-15), Jesus has made his resurrection Spirit available to those who enthrone him as Lord over their life's decisions (Rom. 8:9-14). The exhilaration of living after the Spirit and not after the flesh is reserved for those true believers who have discovered the genuine joy of living like the Lord of life (Rom. 8:1-8). Because of his Spirit's availability to us, striving to live like the Lord of life is infinitely easier than resisting the cross that he calls us all to carry when we decide to follow him. It is both a curse and a blessing that the school of sacrifice never has a recess.

A Christian marriage, more effectively than any other intimate relationship, equips us to be like Christ. Properly understood, it can teach us the ways of God more vividly than any classroom. Marriage is the proving ground for the Church's and the Bible's teaching. It is where our spiritual tires meet the relational road. As Bob Mumford says, the Christian spouse is "married to his school of theology."

When sex and marriage are seen in this context, the fiery trials necessary to purge a Christian couple of their carnal selfishness can be profitably endured. The same flames that burn out emotional impurities fuse a man and woman firmly to each other and can weld them more tightly to their relationship with God. In the process our heavenly Father makes a couple one with him and also with one another.

In this era of chaotic and broken relationships, few things redound more wonderously to the glory of God than a genuinely happy, loving marriage. It's the dream of most, the reality of relatively few. In this instance, as in many others, narrow is the path that leads to life and few there be who find it. Marriage takes us where we'd never choose to go: through the school of sacrifice. But here the ultimate paradox of the gospel reigns: In losing our life we find it. Jesus told us it would be so, and his death and resurrection lucidly illustrate the truth of his message. Whether we listen and learn is up to us.

ELEVEN
SEXUAL DIFFERENCES
AND THEIR
SIGNIFICANCE:
THE SOLUTION
FOR LONELINESS

No culture has ever survived that maintained there are no significant differences between men and women. Feminists are in error when they assert that "there is nothing inherent in the nature of human beings or of society that necessitates that any role or task (save those requiring great strength or the ability to give birth) be associated with one sex or the other."[1] When they maintain that "all the expectations we have of men and women are culturally determined and have nothing to do with any sort of basic male or female nature,"[2] they refuse to examine the facts. It has been undeniably proven by secular scientific research that these assumptions are invalid. To ignore the clear differences that exist between men and women not only jeopardizes individuals and families, but also civilization.

The extraordinary social implications of our sexual differences have not escaped some modern authors. In a novel about ancient Rome, Taylor Caldwell has two of her characters discuss the subtle factors that distinguish a democracy from a republic, and the ways in which each reflects masculine or feminine traits. The ramifications for our society are obvious:

> *Priscus:* "I remember that you told me that Caesars do not seize power; it is thrust upon them by a degenerate people

who have lost their virtue and their strength, and who prefer security to manhood, ease without work, and circuses to duty. . . ."

Lucanus: "You misunderstand me, Priscus. I know that it was inevitable that Rome became what she is. Republics decay into democracies, and democracies degenerate into dictatorships. That fact is immutable. When there is equality—and democracies always bring equality—the people become faceless, they lose power and initiative, they lose pride and independence, they lose their splendor. Republics are masculine, and so they beget the sciences and the arts; they are prideful, heroic and virile. They emphasize God, and glorify Him. But Rome has decayed into a confused democracy, and has acquired feminine traits, such as materialism, greed, the lust for power, and expediency. Masculinity in nations and men is demonstrated by law, idealism, justice and poesy; femininity by materialism, dependence on others, gross emotionalism, and absence of genius. Masculinity seeks what is right; femininity seeks what is immediately satisfying. Masculinity is vision; femininity ridicules vision. A masculine nation produces philosophers, and has a respect for the individual; a feminine nation has an insensate desire to control and dominate. Masculinity is aristocratic; femininity has no aristocracy, and is happy only if it finds about it a multitude of faces resembling it exactly, and a multitude of voices echoing its own sentiments and desires and fears and follies. Rome has become feminine, Priscus. And feminine nations and feminine men inevitably die or are destroyed by a masculine people."

Priscus tried to lighten the subject. He said, jokingly, "My soldiers, the legions of Rome, are no females, Lucanus!" But he frowned and considered. What was a man to do? He was absolutely impotent when the people unanimously preferred soft slavery to hard freedom.[3]

Though all of Taylor Caldwell's gender generalizations are impossible to prove and some are doubtlessly unjustified, she has given us some provocative insights. Let us now consider what the gender lessons of history, religion, and science have to teach us.

OBSERVATIONS FROM THE ANCIENTS AND ANTHROPOLOGY

The Chinese had a unique perspective on gender differences. Their emphasis on the yin and the yang in ancient Taoism saw a symbolic reflection of a creative dualism that was present throughout all of nature. While the unknown authors of their philosophy were probably men and their views contain an obvious masculine bias, it is equally apparent that they would have considered quite absurd the modern feminist view that sexual differences are inconsequential.

Perhaps as early as 1000 B.C., unknown Chinese philosophers "distinguished within every natural object two interacting energy-modes, the *yang* and the *yin*."[4] They believed that everything in existence was constituted by their interplay.

> The yang is described as masculine in character – active, warm, dry, bright, procreative, positive. It is seen in the sun, in anything with heat in it, the south side of a hill, the north side of a river, male properties of all kinds, fire. The yin is an energy-mode in a lower and slower key; it is fertile and breeding, dark, cold, wet, mysterious, secret, the female or negative principle in nature. It is seen in shadows, quiescent things, the north side of a hill, the shadowed south bank of a river.[5]

The Chinese, of course, saw these interacting energy modes as having implications for the interrelationship of men and women. Their judgment of women, as in other primitive cultures, however, is tainted by the Fall. Their women suffered subservience at their hands accordingly. They believed that

> men and women are, not less than inanimate things, the product of the interaction in varying degrees of the yang and the yin. They show differing proportions of the qualities of each activity-mode, men being heavenly (that is, predominantly yang) and of great worth, whereas women earthly (predominantly yin) and of less account.[6]

Expanding on the biblical understanding of the duality of heaven and earth, Taoism talks of *Shen*, which are heavenly spirits, yang in character, and *kuei*, or earthly, yin-like spirits.

Though there are obvious prejudices and imbalances in the Taoistic sexual distinctions, there are also undeniable shades of truth. Especially poignant is their appreciation for the creative dynamic in the interaction of the sexes.

In more recent times anthropological studies of contemporary primitive cultures have yielded some intriguing gems of insight into the significance of gender differences. Perhaps the foremost authority in this area is the famed anthropologist Margaret Mead. She gave much of her life to study the sexuality and gender relationships of primitive peoples.

In her 1949 work, *Male and Female,* Mead made some conclusions concerning the role of gender in behavior, based on her observations of seven remote societies. While her work implies that our traditional gender roles are not universally accepted, a closer investigation of her findings reveals some discoveries that must disappoint modern feminists. In every culture she studied she found the same results:

> There was homicidal violence, and in all, that violence occurred at the hands of men. Tchambuli men may have been effeminate in relation to certain American conventions, but they were still very devoted to taking victims – and, more traditionally, hunting heads. Mundugumor men were unthreatened by having their women provide for them. But that was because it freed them to plot and fight.[7]

Even in cultures where roles appear to be reversed, they are in fact merely different. Mead believed men always maintain their dominance over high-status roles.

Harvard biological anthropologist Melvin Konner observed similar things "in all the world's thousands of different cultures. . . ."

> In every culture there is at least some homicide, in the context of war or ritual or in the context of daily life, and in every culture men are mainly responsible for it. There are, of course, individual exceptions, but there is no society in the ethnographic or historical record in which men do nearly as

much baby and child care as women. This is not to say anything, yet, about capacity; it is merely a statement of plain, observable fact. Men are more violent than women, and women are more nurturant, at least toward infants and children, then men.[8]

The distinction applies even to dreams. In a study of seventy-five tribal societies around the world, "men were more likely to dream of coitus, wife, weapon, animal, red, while women were more likely to dream of husband, mother, father, child, cry."[9]

We will further consider the implications of these findings in the next chapter on sexual roles, but it suffices now to say that men and women are universally different. Men are more prone to violence, women to nurturance. Furthermore, no culture in history has ever acted as if gender roles should be the same. Gender has always influenced destiny and it always will. The only question that remains is whether we as a society will observe godly wisdom in appropriate role differences or whether, here also, we will follow the way that seems right to modern humanity.

SOME SCIENTIFIC SURPRISES

In Dr. Konner's article, "She and He," he summarizes recent scientific data that underscores the undeniable biological differences between men and women. What makes his article all the more compelling is his data – a compilation of conclusions derived from the work of distinguished female scientists. Their reluctant discoveries came as a result of whole lifetimes of work devoted to the study of the brain and hormones, and the behavior of both humans and animals. These women set out to prove that there were no innate differences in the sexes, but were forced to conclude otherwise.

As with Mead's discoveries, the strongest case for gender differences is made in the realm of aggressive behavior. Boys were always shown to be more egotistical and/or aggressive, usually both. They were also usually more dominant, girls more compliant. Cognitively, girls and women are superior in verbal skills, boys and men are stronger in spatial and quantitative ability.[10] Even newborn infants are substantially different. At birth, boys show more muscle strength while girls show greater skin sensitivity, more reflex smiles, more taste sensitivity, more searching movements with their mouths, and faster response to a flash of light.

Some of these behavioral gender differences are attributable to endocrinology-hormonal differences. Others may be related to the different brain structures of men and women. These differences were first proved in 1973, ironically the same time that feminist assertions began to gain widespread recognition – the ones stating that there were no such differences.

To say that these discoveries rocked the neuroscience community is no exaggeration. Dr. Konner himself was a skeptic until he studied the findings of Anke Ehrhardt and her colleagues at the Johns Hopkins School of Medicine. He said, "If not now, then in the very near future, it will be extremely difficult for an informed, objective observer to discard the hypothesis that the genders differ in their degree of violent behavior for reasons that are in part physiological."[11]

Gender differences are being observed by secular researchers in areas that extend far beyond physiology. They permeate the moral realm as well. In *Pastoral Renewal,* psychologist Paul Vitz discusses the results uncovered by Harvard educationist Carol Gilligan's book *In a Different Voice: Psychological Theory and Women's Development.* Her research may offer some insight into the underlying differences between masculine and feminine approaches to problem solving and society alluded to in Taylor Caldwell's novel.

> Gilligan characterizes sex difference in moral thought essentially as follows: men make moral judgments on the basis of abstract principles and rules; women focus on concrete situations and relationships. As a result, men treat moral dilemmas as problems to be solved by sorting out competing principles, regardless of the personal consequences. Women, instead, see moral dilemmas as involving the horizontal network of interpersonal relationships, commitments, obligations, and duties. For women, the moral solution is whatever minimizes the suffering of the particular people involved. This distinction between the sexes might be defined simply: men want justice to prevail; women want mercy to prevail.[12]

Interestingly enough, the twin concepts of mercy and justice are an ancient Hebrew ideal (Prov. 3:3 and elsewhere). They were perfectly balanced in the person of Jesus Christ (John 1:14-17).

WHY WOMAN?

Men and women *are* different. Their differences extend beyond the superior strength of men and the childbearing capacity of women. As was noted, "In almost every feature of their beings, as present-day research continues marvelously to demonstrate, females differ from males: in hormones, nerves, intellectual proclivities, rates and kinds of growth, etc."[13] What significance can be attached to these differences and what are the implications for the relationships of men and women to one another? How do these differences impact sexuality?

To adequately answer these questions, we must turn our attention again to the Scriptures. Specifically, we must begin to answer the question, "Why did God create us male and female?" While this larger question is more adequately explored in the coming chapter on "Spiritual Authority and Social Renewal," it is time to focus our attention on the equally intriguing question: "Why did God create woman?"

For the answer to that question let's again look to the Book of Genesis:

> Now the Lord God said, It is not good [sufficient, satisfactory] that the man should be alone; I will make him a helper meet [suitable, adapted, completing] for him. . . . And the Lord God caused a deep sleep to fall upon Adam, and while he slept He took one of his ribs—a part of his side—and closed up the [place with] flesh instead of it; and the rib or part of his side which the Lord God had taken from the man, He built up and made into a woman and brought her to the man. Then Adam said, This [creature] is now bone of my bones and flesh of my flesh. She shall be called Woman, because she was taken out of a man. Therefore a man shall leave his father and his mother and shall become united and cleave to his wife, and they shall become one flesh. And the man and his wife

111

were both naked, and were not embarrassed or ashamed in each other's presence. (Gen. 2:18, 21-25, AMP.)

Few people would deny that loneliness is indeed one of life's saddest and most pervasive problems. This passage from Genesis teaches us that God is concerned about man's loneliness. He characteristically acted to satisfy that need. His perfect solution for man's loneliness? Woman! It would appear that man was largely created to have fellowship with God, whereas woman was created for the purpose of relationship with man.

Looking around at all the lonely people, both within and outside of marriage, we might well ask if the Lord really knew what he was doing. The escalating battle of the sexes and the current trend toward homosexuality add further credence to the question: How can woman be the perfect solution for man's loneliness if all these problems persist?

The answer may lie in our thorough misunderstanding of the purpose the Lord intended for the male-female relationship.

To understand how men and women can perfectly complement one another and live in a manner that is mutually fulfilling and harmonious, we must properly discern the function God intended for men and women to have in their relationship to each other. Only then can we discover how the Creator intended for us to serve as the solution to one another's loneliness; only then can we find the key to happy and harmonious sexual relationships. God is a God of relationships. He created people to live in a loving, ordered, harmonious relationship both with their Creator and with creation. To that end, God created humans, male and female, after his own likeness and image.

The implication behind this statement is that God is both male and female. This is not to deny the importance of relating to God as our (masculine) Father. If we would understand the proper functioning of men and women, however, we must see that because humans were made male and female after God's image, our wholeness is best enhanced through the growth that occurs when we unite in a covenant relationship with one of the opposite sex. The complete image of God is both male and female.

If a man and woman would overcome their own brokenness and alienation, if they would achieve a greater sense of wholeness and completeness, the best way—the most efficient way for them to do that—is through their union with God and one another. The sense of unity and oneness with their Creator and their spouses is one into which they will grow as they faithfully fulfill their covenant obligations to one another in a godly marital relationship.

Once a man and woman have eternally covenanted themselves together for their mutual highest good, they can, with God's help, learn to redemptively resolve the inevitable conflicts that arise from their sexual and personality differences. In such a relationship the nurturing tendencies of the woman will tend to moderate the more dominant tendencies in the man. Similarly, the aggressive inclinations of the man, properly channeled and controlled, will help to protect the woman from her own vulnerability and tendency to be overly compassionate.

It is important to note here that the Creator infused both the man and the woman with the proper chemistry and makeup to enable them to fulfill their God-ordained functions and roles. The additional testosterone that makes a man masculine gives him the superior strength he needs to fulfill his role as protector and provider. It is not without a cost, however. The man usually wears out his body at an earlier age than the woman, and dies much younger. Similarly the woman's more nurturing traits naturally prepare her for her major role as mother of her children and helpmate to her husband.

When a man and woman understand their natural differences in light of scriptural roles, they have a better opportunity to work cooperatively with the Creator toward the happiness and fulfillment he has ordained for them. They can work together with a better understanding of their unique strengths and weaknesses, cooperating instead of competing.

Scriptural principles, examples, and constrictions can keep men and women from indulging their own harmful inclinations contrary to the well-being of each other and their offspring.

The bearing and raising of children is another important reason for gender differences. Children need both a mother and a father. As Charles Simpson says, when a child falls and hurts himself, Mom tends to say, "Poor thing," while Dad exhorts him not to bleed on the rug! There is both a time for compassion and a need to overcome self-pity. And as Bob Mumford observes, between a mom and a dad, the child usually gets a good pair of parents. Children raised without the distinctive input of both a mother and father usually find it more difficult to make a healthy adjustment to adult life.

It is important to realize that, because of the Fall and modern trends away from a biblical understanding of sexual roles and responsibilities, there are many abnormal relationships. Because of the devastating divorce rate and increased sexual irresponsibility in our society, many people have lived with the reality of absentee or delinquent fathers. Many sons do not have the sufficient role models to become the righteous heads-of-family needed in their own households. Many women, by default, have had to carry burdens they should never have had to shoulder. The result is a deformed perspective of men, women, and family relationships. That twisted reality must not be allowed to warp our view of God's best.

The only solution is a return to scriptural norms. When we realize that the Word of God does indeed endure forever (Isa. 40:8) and that its teachings on sexual differences are normative throughout history (1 Cor. 14:34-38), we can embrace them as foundational for our own lives and families. God's Word can shape us to overcome our environmental family deficiencies. When we also see that the Creator's teachings in this crucial area are thoroughly consistent with our chemical makeup and his purposes, we find in them the key to our well-being and to the emotional health of our children and all of society.

SEXUAL DIFFERENCES AND THE SEX ACT

The differences between men and women don't stop here, however. The impact of our sexual differences on the sex act itself is profound; the potential for misunderstanding those differences, frightening. For men, sex is more of an isolated physical phenomenon than it is for women. Most men find it relatively easy to divorce sex from love. Most women, however, relate more emotionally to sex. It is generally more difficult for them to enjoy or even participate in sex unless their heart or emotions are stirred. Since a woman usually has much more to lose if an irresponsible sexual relationship produces an undesired offspring, the woman's need for love and security in order to enjoy sex seems to be a built-in form of self-protection.

One manifestation of these differences is seen in the predominantly female interest in soap operas. It has been said that the soaps are the only place in which men are as interested in relationships as women. Romantic, vicarious involvement in these daytime fantasies can feed a strong emotional craving in a woman in the same way that pornography fuels the lust in men's hearts. Perhaps it could be said of pornography, predominantly a male phenomenon, that it is the only place in which women are as interested in sex as men are.

Preoccupation with either romance or sensuality can lead people into unhealthy dissatisfaction with their mates; dissatisfaction that forebodes potential problems and threats to the marriage. Evidence strongly implying that different sexual priorities in men and women are inherent was unearthed in modern studies of homosexuals. It was found that the *average* homosexual male experienced sex with more than five hundred different partners in his lifetime. Lesbians, however, were less interested in physical gratification alone and more apt to seek deeper emotional involvement. Lesbians averaged only five different sexual partners in the course of a lifetime.[14] Both male and female homosexuals apparently find monogamous relationships to be extremely difficult if not impossible to maintain.

One can see how the failure of men and women to understand the sexual perspectives of the opposite sex can lead to their inability to relate to, understand, and satisfy one another's needs. Our trend toward an androgynous (unisex) society – one that minimizes the differences between men and women – only further distorts the problem. It is evident that some men and women become disillusioned about love relationships with the opposite sex. Some individuals even seek out members of their own sex who can better understand and fulfill their superficial needs.

The problem with homosexuality, however, is that it doesn't lead to the deep and lasting satisfaction God intended when he created us male and female as a perfect complement to one another. Don Williams, author of *The Homosexual Matrix*, observes that healthy heterosexual relationships are "rich in tension and stimulating contrasts" as opposed to homosexual relationships which are "overclose, fatigue prone, and are often adjusted to narrow, trigger-sensitive tolerances."[15]

I am in no way saying that marriage between a man and woman guarantees them a deep, full, satisfying relationship. Obviously this is not the case. Some married couples do not understand each other and their needs well enough to make their marriages fulfilling. However, a biblically ordered relationship between a man and a woman has potential for completeness and satisfaction that will be impossible for a homosexual or lesbian couple to obtain.

How can this be true? How is it that men and women in relationship to one another can aspire to a level of satisfaction that is impossible for homosexual couples to achieve? How is it that the opposite sex truly is the solution to our loneliness and the key to our completion as persons formed after the image and likeness of God?

While it may be possible for a woman to understand and serve another woman's emotional needs effectively, and likewise for a man to serve another man's sexual urges efficiently, these acts will never lead a homosexual couple to the depth of fulfillment that God intended for men and women to achieve in their relationship to one another. Because we are made to be like the God who is unselfish love, we will only find our deepest satisfaction in being like him. The selfish gratification of our instinctual urges can never replace the deeper satisfaction that can be attained only by learning how to love genuinely and unselfishly.

God created us male and female not only so that together we could reflect his image, but also so that through one another men and women could be drawn beyond themselves and learn how to love. More important, through a proper biblical understanding of male-female relationships, we see a reflection of the magnanimous nature and quality of love that the Lord has for his people. He is our heavenly Husband. His bride is the Church. In his relationship to us he serves as an eternal prototype, showing us how to bring heaven to earth in our sexual relationships.

Comprehending, receiving, and yielding in obedience to God's love is the secret to all human fulfillment. Without his fullness dwelling within our hearts, human life remains empty. Without his truth to guide us and grace to empower us, we all live lives not only of quiet desperation but also of anxious meaninglessness.

In vivid contrast to the dogma of the human potential movement's constant exhortations to save our own lives and sanctify our selfish impulses is this simple yet profound paradox which Jesus exposed. He said that he who wishes to save his life will lose it, but whoever loses his own life for his sake will find salvation, wholeness, and complete fulfillment: "Unless a grain of wheat falls into the earth and dies, it remains by itself alone; but if it lives, it bears much fruit" (John 12:24). Is it not the reluctance to die to ourselves that is the principle cause of our loneliness and meaningless pursuits? The easy way, the natural path, is seldom, if ever, the one that leads to the greatest rewards.

Because most men have not been sensitive or responsive to women's deeper needs, many women have swallowed the feminist propaganda wholeheartedly. Leaving behind home and family, they have sought to find, through competition with men, the love and satisfaction that seem so elusive in the rough-and-tumble give and take of family life. Similarly many men, disillusioned with wives who use sex as a bartering tool, have pursued the forbidden fruit of the playboy philosophy. They hope through the sexual subjugation of many partners to find the ego gratification that seems beyond their grasp in a relationship with one woman.

Both of these courses are doomed to fail. Perhaps the reason is best summed up in this lucid and starkly realistic statement from Michael Novak:

> In our society, of course, there is no need to become an adult. One may remain — one is daily exhorted to remain — a child forever. In such a life, the central aim is self-fulfillment. Marriage is merely an alliance, entailing as minimal an abridgment of inner privacy as one partner may allow. Children are not a welcome responsibility, for to have children is, plainly, to cease being a child oneself. One tries instead to live as the angels were once believed to live — soaring, free, unencumbered.
>
> People say of marriage that it is boring, when what they mean is that it terrifies them: too many and too deep are its soaring revelations, its angers, its rages, its hates, and its loves. They say of marriage that it is deadening, when what they mean is that it drives us beyond adolescent fantasies and romantic dreams. They say of children that they are piranhas, brats, snots, when what they mean is that the importance of parents with respect to the future of their children is now known with greater clarity and exactitude than ever before.
>
> Being married and having children has impressed on my mind certain lessons, and most of what I am forced to learn

about myself is not pleasant. The quantity of sheer impenetrable selfishness in the human breast (in *my* breast) is a never-failing source of wonderment. I do not want to be disturbed, challenged, troubled. Huge regions of myself belong only to me. Seeing myself through the unblinking eyes of an intelligent, honest spouse is humiliating. Trying to act fairly to children, each of whom is temperamentally different from myself and from each other, is baffling. My family bonds hold me back from many opportunities. And yet these bonds are, I know, my liberation. They force me to be a different sort of human being in a way I want and need.[16]

Through the act of marriage we become more like Christ who is the embodiment of unselfish love. We can be true to who we really are only in proportion to our ability to become like him. It is to that end – our ultimate wholeness as men and women fashioned after God's image – that he has ordained the intimate interaction of the sexes in marriage.

Who are we really meant to be? We are to be loving, giving persons who resemble Christ and show the love of our Creator. Marriage provides God's setting for us to loose the bonds of our own selfishness and free us to be our real selves.

Through the woman, the man can be freed from the frustrating shackles of his own lusts and learn the deeper, more genuine satisfactions of an intimate relationship.

Through the man, the woman can become liberated from the tyranny of her own emotions and integrate her inner heart craving with a deep, full, bodily response to the love and tenderness of her husband.

This process will require that both partners learn to deny their own appetites and needs for the sake of their mates; but is this really such a sacrifice? Total abandonment to one's needs and wants lead only to despair; it can never bring satisfaction. On the other hand, someone who subordinates his or her needs for the sake of a mate's learns life's most valuable lesson. That person learns how to love unselfishly. Life is no longer merely a playground. Rather, that person's marriage becomes the classroom of the eternal God who is love.

Again we see that the person who learns to love finds the secret of a rich, full life. Conversely, those who opt instead for the seemingly easier route of pursuing their own pleasures guarantee their own unhappiness. Pleasure as an end in itself is self-defeating. Unmitigated selfishness, ironically, is counterproductive. Pursuit of it can never lead to happiness or fulfillment but only to an inner emptiness and an obsession with the trivial, the superficial, and the sensual—all in a vain attempt to find acceptance and satisfaction.

God knew precisely what he was doing when he made us male and female—uniquely different from one another. It was his eternal wisdom that dictated his creation of woman as the solution to man's loneliness. Those who learn the sublime truths related to God's love, based on the biblical model of male-female relationships, find the eternal solution for their aloneness and alienation. They also discover the secret of an abundant and harmonious relationship with their mate.

Those who glean these insights from the Scriptures take a giant step forward. Loving unselfishly, they will be almost certain to have a rich, full life; a life that becomes a foretaste of a blissful eternity; a life of learning how to truly love another person. Through the knowledge thus gained comes a deeper, fuller understanding of the Creator's self-sacrificing love for us, his creatures.

TWELVE
FEMINISM'S
FATAL FLAWS

However, each one of you also must love his wife as he loves himself, and the wife must respect her husband (Eph. 5:33, NIV).

If anybody thinks he is a prophet or spiritually gifted, let him acknowledge that what I am writing to you is the Lord's command. If he ignores this, he himself will be ignored. (1 Cor. 14:37-38)

The Russian philosopher Berdyaev said, "The idea of woman's emancipation is based upon a profound enmity between the sexes, upon envy and imitation. Woman becomes a mere caricature, a pseudo-being."[1]

This probably explains why feminism is failing. It may be succeeding at dramatically altering our society and the lives of many people, but for the most part it is making their lives worse instead of better. This was to be expected. In an article entitled "The Androgyny Hoax," the writing of Ferdinand Lundberg and Marynia Farnham, M.D., anticipated these consequences. In analyzing the book entitled *Modern Woman: The Lost Sex*, the article states:

The authors reserved their sharpest words for feminists. Such activists, they said, sought not justice but masculinity. "And a female who attempts to achieve masculinity is psychically ill in the same way as a male who attempts to achieve femininity." Feminists feared and despised children, Lundberg and Farnham reported, and pursued an ideology that was "the very negation of femaleness." Insofar as feminists achieved their goal, "it spelled only vast individual suffering for men as well as women, and much public disorder."[2]

The quality of life in today's culture is eroding, and part of the reason why is that the feminist philosophy is fatally flawed.

The well-intentioned people who embrace a feminist philosophy never intended these things, but the results of their dubious sociological experiment are anything but promising. Ironically and sadly, those who have suffered most from its upheavals are usually the very women it most sought to help.

WHY FEMINISM?

It's easy to understand why feminism caught on as it did. For much of my life I, too, thought that it was the only just and righteous perspective to have. Shortly after my conversion, when I first read about biblical sexual roles, they seemed archaic and unfair—a throwback to a primitive age when men ruled everything and women were considered inferior. It took me a while to comprehend the wisdom in the Bible's approach. As with many kingdom principles (turn the other cheek, love your enemy, overcome evil with good, etc.), Scripture's superior insights were not immediately evident to my carnal mind.

That many modern women should be deceived by feminist philosophies is no surprise; I am often amazed that more women have not been so seduced. Men abdicated their familial responsibilities years ago. In large numbers they abandoned home and hearth to pursue the almighty dollar. It is remarkable that it took women so long to follow them.

HOW DID IT ALL BEGIN?

At one time, a woman's presence in the home was absolutely vital to her family's well-being. As recently as the turn of the century, it took as much energy for a woman to wash, cook, and clean as it took for the average man to bring home the bacon. Her efforts were every bit as essential to the survival of the family as his. Her value and contributions to the home and family were unquestioned. Church and society affirmed the worth of her calling. Young women aspired to be excellent mothers and homemakers.

In that period, men may have seldom washed the dishes or changed the diapers, but they certainly appreciated the women who did. Most men did all they could to faithfully provide their families with the essentials and any added comforts that could make their lives easier. The man's role as provider was similarly cherished and affirmed by society. It was undergirded by our laws and mores. It was widely recognized that the man ought to provide for his own. If he didn't, he was worse than an infidel (1 Tim. 5:8).

Providing meant more than mere bacon-bringing, however. It also meant involvement with the children, both in their care and discipline, and also in their recreation. Without radio and television and other sophisticated forms of social escape, families picnicked and played together. Games, worship, winter outings, work around the homestead and trips to the circus, beach, and ballpark were carefully woven into the fabric of everyday life. People did things together as a family. Divorce was almost unheard of, adultery rare, and other sexual practices which are destructive of family life and the social fiber were virtually unthinkable.

Perhaps most significant is that men were regarded every bit as necessary to the family's well-being as were women. Men's unique role as godly husbands and fathers was encouraged by the laws, values, and traditions of our society, which were patterned after scriptural precepts and standards. Fatherhood and motherhood were both infused with the dignity, significance, and worth they deserved.

The trickle-down effect of the industrial revolution that made modern conveniences readily available to the masses helped to subtly undermine this family-social structure. Women's homemaking didn't seem as necessary as it had been. The rise of modern science, and the growing humanistic behavioral views that contended with scriptural standards for the hearts and minds of our people, accelerated the erosion of family-oriented roles and values. The devastation of two world wars and the tidal wave of prosperity that followed in their wake fostered a further polarization of the family. The increasingly irresponsible influences of the mass media, with its worldly, elite, male-dominated, hedonistic views of sex, family, and violence only sped up the process. By the time the sexual revolution began to devastate the value structure of our society, there was little left to resist it. Even certain misguided segments of the American church embraced its "enlightened"[3] and sophisticated deceptions.

The net result of all these social evolutions? Many women no longer felt significant at home. Instead they felt neglected and even scorned for desiring to stay there. Though it is much harder to commit oneself to learning to be a good mother, wife, and home-maker than to prepare for almost any other career, this choice in life has been subordinated to a view that demands that a woman prove her worth and authenticate her existence in the same way as a man: through a career away from the home, making money and even engaging in illicit sexual conquests.

The feminists' denigration of the role of wife and mother was no accident. Those whose writings became the foundation of the modern feminist revolution intended this; it is consistent with their political and ideological goals. In 1970 Shulamith Firestone elaborated on the logical conclusion of the feminist agenda. Assuming that the Communist Revolution in Russia was sputtering because of its failure to destroy the nuclear family, she concluded that " 'Mom' is vital to the American way of life, considerably more than apple pie. She is an institution without which the system would really fall apart. Hence, 'Mom' must be eliminated, to be supplanted by a 'feminist socialism' that would end capitalist exploitation."[4] The attempt to decimate the American family and thus usher in a socialistic feminist utopia would have a profound impact on men.

Many men would no longer consider their roles as husbands and fathers as significant contributions to an ordered society and to the future of the world. It is easier to get divorced than married, to philander than to remain faithful, to succeed at making money than to be an effective father and husband. Society indicates that many "real men" refuse to be shackled to responsibility, can never be satisfied with one woman for a lifetime, and thrive on vicarious adventure and violence. Children are viewed as a drag, and the man who has too many is considered an undisciplined boob who doesn't care about society.

Ironically, the feminists' attempts to help women who have been hardened and abused by renegade men and delinquent fathers have only made it probable that there will be more such women. As feminists have sought to guarantee that a woman won't be vocationally or economically vulnerable to men, men have felt less necessary in their roles as responsible husbands and fathers. Consequently they have flown the coop with greater frequency. When they haven't abandoned their families, they have brutishly assumed that their wives should earn as much money as possible. Many are the wives who have come to me, desperate to trade their "liberation" for the privilege of being full-time mothers, but their husbands wouldn't hear of it.

A friend of mine, responsible for the hiring of managers in a local factory, needed to add thirty new supervisors. To his chagrin, in our economically depressed region he could find only fifteen men willing to take these full-time positions. The others that he interviewed told him they didn't want year-round jobs. Since their wives "worked" they were only interested in seasonal jobs where they would be laid off six months a year and could hunt in the winter and fish in the summer.

Feminist values have made it seem necessary for many insecure men to validate their own gender in these irresponsible ways and predominantly masculine pursuits. The man who expects his wife to shoulder the load financially is seldom likely to raise a hand to help her with the housework. The feminist's illusion of an ideal man – one who is willing to assume half of the wifely duties at home and enable her to find "real fulfillment" outside the home – is an unrealistic vision that even women's magazines are admitting will probably never become a reality in most marriages.

IS THIS THE FEMINIST UTOPIA?

Is there evidence that the feminist social revolution has actually harmed women? Or better, we might ask, has it helped nearly as many as it has harmed? Feminism has enabled an elite upper and upper-middle class few to find prestigious jobs they would not otherwise have sought. But the large majority of women are paying a heavy price for these benefits.

The data I'll be referring to comes from the federal government's *Statistical Abstracts of the United States*. I looked to this source for objective information because I believed that if the obliteration of sexual roles was indeed contrary to God's will, as the Scriptures indicate, then there would be evidence that society's trend in this direction has brought about negative changes in the quality of life for women. These changes, I felt, would be so profound as to be reflected in various statistical measurements that would serve as a barometer for the life quality of women in America during the years these changes took place.

Sure enough, the statistical evidence was overwhelming. In every area I looked, life was becoming harder, more burdensome, and less problem-free for women. This was especially true over the past two decades, when feminism so dramatically altered our perception of women and their roles. While it is impossible to blame feminism for all the problems women have encountered during the past twenty years, it is equally impossible to deny its negative impact. Feminism, more than any other factor, has influenced the status and perception of women during this period. It must assume a substantial portion of the blame for the resulting suffering of many women.

One notorious fact in recent years is the escalating divorce rate. While divorce is devastating to all parties involved, it is particularly problematic for women. It is much harder for them to become separated from their children. They are usually more closely bonded to their offspring than men are. Consequently they have a much harder time earning a decent living, thus plunging themselves and their families into poverty. I was recently told that over 90 percent of the people on welfare in our area are single-parent families headed by women. I expect this is also true elsewhere. All this human suffering is the bitter fruit of the early taproots of the modern feminist movement.

One feminist writes that "the end of the institution of marriage is a necessary condition for the liberation of women" and that they "must work to destroy it. . . ."[5] Evidence suggests they've been partially successful in achieving that goal. While marriages per thousand have remained fairly constant throughout the century (10.3 in 1910, 10.1 in 1977, 10.5 in 1984), the divorce rate during the same period increased manifold, especially at the height of feminist influence in the late seventies. This increase has accelerated so dramatically in recent years that the increase in the divorce rate from 1965-1977 outpaced the increase that occurred in the fifty-five

126

years prior to that. There were .9/1,000 in 1910, 2.5/1,000 in 1965, 5.0/1,000 in 1977, and 4.9/1,000 in 1984. That's more than a 500 percent increase in this century. From 1950-1965 the rate had begun to decline, but with the upsurge of feminist influence it exploded from 1965 on. The divorce rate per 1,000 marriages went from 9.2 in 1960 to 10.6 in 1965, 14.9 in 1970, and 22.6 in 1981, more than doubling during the period when feminism really came into its own. A slight decline in 1982 to 21.7/1,000 parallels the waning of feminist influences in the eighties and a renewed appreciation for marriage and committed, traditional relationships.

Another statistic reflecting the toll that all this marital chaos has exacted is the number of mother-only households. In 1960, 7.4 percent of the households in the United States with minor children were headed by females with no spouse present. By 1970 that figure had climbed to 10.2 percent. By 1980 it had jumped to 17.6 percent, more than doubling in less than twenty years. As of 1984 it had continued to climb to 19 percent. Women and their children must pay the most for the tragic erosion of male responsibility that has been unwittingly precipitated by the changing perceptions of sexual roles. They are the ones most often plunged into poverty and left emotionally wounded and relationally handicapped by the absence of a responsible husband and father.

According to these same *Statistical Abstracts* there's also been an alarming rise in violence during the same years. Again, women have usually been the greatest victims. From 1967 to 1970 violent rapes increased 37 percent; by 1975, 103 percent; and by 1977 a disastrous 128 percent. Does feminism have anything to do with this? There are two ways in which it may.

First, feminism sought to erode the sexual double-standard between men and women. This made "sexiness" a desirable trait. The girls I dated in high school and college in the late sixties would have been insulted if I had told them they were sexy. Many young women today would accept that as a compliment. Hence women dress, act, and talk sexier. This may have even helped to open the door for the flood of increasingly explicit and violent pornography that has swept our nation in the last twenty years.

Few women understand that visual stimuli affect a man the way tactile stimuli affects a woman. What is just a new fashion to a girl can be interpreted as an open invitation to a red-blooded teenage boy, a veritable provocation to a sex-starved, perverted young man. Demented men, like the Son of Sam serial killer in New York some years ago, leave a bedroom full of pornography behind and hit the streets seeking vengeance against all women who dangle their wares before his eyes. All this kind of man knows is that women never let him have what he looked at and lusted after.

We should be concerned, however, with more than just serial killers. Some startling statistics in recent years reveal a sharp rise (25 percent) in the "acquaintance" rapes of college coeds during dates. The young men who commit these crimes more often say they only took what they had coming to them.

Most experts concur that rape is motivated more by aggression against women than by overt sexual drives. The radical feminists who so flagrantly flaunted their hatred and disrespect for men during the feminist rallies of the sixties and seventies may have seldom felt the fury they unleashed in many unstable, frustrated males, but, as these statistics show, other women certainly have.

It is impossible to sow seeds of hatred, violence, and abuse and not expect to reap a harvest in like kind. The violent inclinations of men, untempered by biblical values or satisfying, responsible marriage relationships, have often been ventilated on women who were defenseless against men's pent-up rage.

After the Fall the tendency toward violence became a particularly masculine problem. But when the feminist movement encouraged divorce as a solution to marital problems and did so much to foster an unsubmissive attitude in women toward their husbands, it helped make domestic violence the national tragedy it has become today. Much feminist literature has encouraged women to express their rage. In the furnace of a heated marital hassle this has only served to add fuel to the fire causing much untold suffering both for women and men. Some of these hurting men would rather kill their wives than lose them.

Unfortunately, the problems don't stop here. The *Statistical Abstracts* reveal a dramatic escalation during this period in the drug abuse and alcohol dependency rate among women. There was a similarly steep climb in the rate of suicides and violent crimes committed by women. About the only index that declined was life expectancy, but that is not surprising. When life is increasingly stressful, the quality of health declines.

Is it fair to blame feminism for these destructive trends in modern life? Though radical feminists saw marriage as a woman's problem and divorce her solution, it was never the intention of the majority of women involved in the liberation movement to encourage divorce or to foster an atmosphere where rape, violence, suicide, and chemical dependency increased. To be sure, other factors have collided with our culture, including the erosion of Judeo-Christian values, the sexual revolution, the proliferation of pornography, and the flight from personal responsibility.

Life in the shadow of nuclear annihilation, the rise of television and with it surrealistic media violence, a shorter work week, and our unprecedented prosperity have all been factors in the problems reflected in these statistics. A significant portion of the blame, however, must be shared by those who, with good intentions, naively encouraged the disintegration of role distinctions. No other factor of modern life has so dramatically altered the lives of women or shaped their approach to life's most significant relationships.

SEXUAL SUICIDE

One man who has an excellent grasp of the consequences of the "sexual suicide" we are committing is George Gilder.[6] His book by that title made him an early enemy of the feminist movement, but his eloquent reasoning has yet to be refuted. It has merely been ignored by most. The problems he prophesied early on in the feminist revolution are coming to pass.

Gilder's premise is that role distinctions are necessary for the well-being of men, children and society, but most of all for the sake of women. Gilder maintains that by nature of the intimate involvement of women's bodies with the whole act of reproduction, they are almost inextricably involved with their offspring. This may help to explain their obvious nurturing tendencies. This factor not only makes desertion of the family much more difficult for a woman than for a man, but, more important, it makes the gratification of her ego needs far more natural. Furthermore, it simplifies her self-authentication as a sexual being. Each month, whether she bears children or not, every woman is reminded of her femininity.

A man's sexuality is not so obvious. Not only is his body not intimately involved with carrying and nurturing children, but neither does he have an "automatic" and consistent way of proving his masculinity. Furthermore, there is nothing that serves, as childbirth does for a woman, to perpetuate his life and give him a sense of immortality – of life and significance beyond his own achievements. The result of this is that he has ego needs, aggravated, I might add, by his more aggressive chemical makeup. This superior strength and inclination toward violence in men was a necessary feature when a man had to protect his family against wild beasts and other primitive perils. In our modern world, however, it leaves him with an untapped reservoir of potent ego needs and a capacity for physical violence that must be sublimated and constructively gratified if the man is to have a full and satisfying life.

Gilder would argue that, up until the last two decades, society was so structured as to reinforce men's necessary position of responsibility. The inequities built into the work force were designed as an incentive for a man to work to support the family he had propagated. In Gilder's estimation this also reinforced the man's role and made it feasible for him to derive ego gratification from the things that would cause him to remain responsibly involved with his family. If we remove the intentionally and carefully constructed biases built into society to affirm and support distinct sexual roles, Gilder postulated, men would have to search elsewhere beyond the family for their sense of worth, sexual validation, and self-authentication.

Gilder predicted that the result of the suicide of sexual distinctions would ultimately be the deterioration of family life. Actually this is thoroughly consistent with the goals of the strong lesbian influence in the feminist movement. Speaking for them, Ann Ferguson wrote, "If the sexual division of labor were destroyed, the mechanism that trains boys and girls to develop heterosexual identities would also be destroyed . . . [and] bisexuality would then be the norm rather than the exception."[7]

The present nuclear family, which was seen as "the source of reproduction of heterosexuality," could be "overturned" very simply. Women needed to secure "equal social, economical and political power outside the home." If "bottle-baby technologies" (the means of producing test-tube babies) were to be perfected and the Supreme Court persuaded to decide that it is unconstitutional to teach or reinforce heterosexuality in the schools, the success of this androgynous agenda would be assured.[8]

Gilder realized, however, that if the nuclear family were "overturned," it would cause the inevitable proliferation of social problems that could ultimately decay our civilization. Certainly this has been the pattern of previous "advanced" cultures, and it would appear to be what is happening today. Psychologist Paul Vitz says, "Male rejection of this principle of commitment [to love, protect, and provide for his family] is the primary source of our widespread family and social pathology." He goes on to say, "In many respects, the pathology of radical feminism is best understood as a reaction to the earlier rejection by men of interpersonal responsibility."[9] I don't believe a radical feminist exists in America today who had a good relationship with both parents or who had or currently has a healthy, permanent relationship with men. In effect they are afflicting a whole society with the unresolved pain of their own past hurts.

Some of the matriarchs of modern feminism sought to supplant our family structures with a social order more conducive to what Shulamith Firestone called "its natural polymorphously perverse sexuality."[10] Andrea Dworkin said that the nuclear family – "the school of values in a sexist, sexually repressed society" – must also be crushed. Turning to positive models, Dworkin saw homosexuality as closer to the androgynous vision. Better still was bestiality, where "human and other-animal relationships would become more explicitly erotic." The destruction of the incest taboo was also essential to "the free-flow of natural androgynous eroticism." Children were "erotic beings, closer to androgyny than the adults who oppress them," and deserving of "every right to live out their own erotic impulses." The overall goal was cultural transformation, "the development of a new kind of human being and a new kind of human community."[11]

Through a smoke screen of misunderstandings (attached to a catalog of valid grievances against a society increasingly dominated by irresponsible and insensitive men), the women's liberation movement has seduced many people away from biblical principles. These standards were designed by our Creator to steer us away from all this unnecessary hurt and guarantee the well-being of men, women, families, and society. His vision for a new society, the kingdom of God come to earth, is a far more promising one.

WHY ARE SEXUAL ROLES NECESSARY?

We must, at this point, ask ourselves why sexual roles are necessary in today's society. We must also deal with the issue of alleged male superiority. Does the Bible's teaching concerning women's roles in the church and at home infer that women are inferior?

Though some prominent but mistaken theologians through Church history did believe that women were inferior, this is not the Bible's rationale for the biblically defined role of women. The Bible recognizes that, in general, women are physically weaker than men. The Bible teaches that women can be emotionally vulnerable, more so than men (1 Pet. 3:7); women tend to think with their hearts while men feel with their brains. Both sexes need each other.

Beyond all basic and significant differences, however, there is one underlying reason why it is in the best interests of women to affirm the social tradition of women's subordination: Life has been better for women under the influence of Christian culture and traditions than under any other societal influence. In Hinduism a woman was "merely a body for the sexual pleasure of a husband, condemned to burn on the funeral pyre if he should die first, which itself would be attributable to some omission on her part."[12] Outside many Moslem mosques there used to be a sign saying Women, Dogs, and Other Impure Animals Not Permitted.[13] Even Orthodox Jews were once taught to thank God daily that they were not born female. But where biblical Christianity has flourished, women have been treated with greater love and respect than under any other cultural influence.

The reason is simple. To summarize, the Bible teaches that men should cherish, nurture, protect, and lovingly lead their wives. It also teaches that men must relate to their wives as Christ relates to his body of believers and cares about their needs and desires. Furthermore, it teaches that men must be responsible for their families and do all they can to provide for their well-being. Nature dictates that in battles based on physical strength, women most often lose. Yet a proper understanding of submission,[14] which we will explore further, gives a woman the same sort of equalizing moral ability that judo and the martial arts give a physically smaller opponent, thus allowing one to use an opponent's weight to gain a victory that would otherwise be impossible. A wise woman would never use this biblical insight manipulatively, but righteously to better serve the Lord and advance his kingdom. She would know that relating to her husband in Christ's way is ultimately in her own best interests, and that doing so from a right spirit will be blessed. Wise indeed is the woman who can see beyond the surface rhetoric of the feminists' arguments, and, in light of the facts reflected in society, can have insight into the Scriptures and her own life in relationship with men, realizing that God has the best way for her to live.

Just as restoration with God is necessary for an individual to be made whole and his life to make sense, so also is a restoration of biblical roles necessary to restore marriage, the family, society, and individuals to a place of solid relational health.

BIBLICAL SEXUAL ROLES AND HOW THEY WORK

What exactly is the biblical view of sexual roles? How do they work? Probably the most complete and concise answers to these questions are found in the familiar passage in Ephesians 5. Portions of this passage are used in many marriage ceremonies, and the instruction it offers has been the foundation for the Christian view of marriage. Properly understood, Ephesians 5 contains the counsel necessary to teach a man and woman how to have the marriage of their dreams.

Unfortunately, many Bible teachers do not mention that Ephesians 5 starts out by advocating mutual submission: "Submit to one another out of reverence for Christ" (Eph. 5:21, NIV). Though the Bible teaches that Christian women are to submit to their husbands, it is nevertheless both prudent and realistic in its requirement for a husband and wife to be subject to one another out of reverence for Christ. The Christian—man or woman—is to be subject to Christ and to pattern his or her life after him. Jesus clearly taught that biblical authority is rooted not in heavy-handedness but in servanthood. The greatest must be as the least (Matt. 20:25-28). Our happiness depends on our learning to follow Christ's example of subjection and humility toward those he led (John

13:12-17). His model of servanthood, however, is one of a father's disciplinary concern for his children. Though never heavy-handed, it recognizes that peace at any price is too expensive.

The passage from Ephesians goes on to specify the particular things expected of each mate. First, women are addressed: "Wives, be subject—be submissive and adapt yourselves—to your own husbands as [a service] to the Lord" (Eph. 5:22, AMP.). Notice it does not say the wife should submit because her husband is always right or always deserves it. She is to do it as a service to Jesus. Why? "For the husband is head of the wife as Christ is the Head of the church, Himself the Savior of [His] body" (v. 23). The woman was subjected to the man as a consequence of the Fall. This was done because she was the one who was deceived and sinned first (1 Tim. 2:14). As Christ through his Word guides his earthly body, the Church, away from things it desires that are contrary to its own good, so also the husband is commanded to lead the wife.

The next verse highlights the importance of a woman marrying the right man: "As the church is subject to Christ, so also the wives ought to be to their husbands in everything." How is the wife to be subject to her husband? To what extent should she carry this submission? She is instructed to be subject to him as the Church is subject to Christ. It is interesting to note the fact that the word *lord* is synonymous with *husband* in the Old Testament.

In this age of women's rights many women are uncomfortable if they find themselves married to men who refuse to lead them. I recall a television program on changing sexual roles that told of a woman who had left her husband and child for a successful career in broadcasting. She was intent upon not marrying again unless she found someone more successful who could "make her feel like a woman." Her example indicates how most women don't really like to hold the reins of the marriage relationship. These paradoxical feelings were accurately described by the young wife whose message to men was as follows:

> Don't yield your leadership, that's the main thing. Don't hand us the reins. We would consider this an abdication on your part. It would confuse us, it would alarm us, it would make us draw back. Quicker than anything else, it will fog the clear vision that made us love you in the first place. Oh, we will try to get you to give up your position as Number One in

the house. That is the terrible contradiction in us. We will seem to be fighting you to the last ditch for final authority, but in the obscure recesses of our hearts we want you to win. You have to win, for we aren't made for leadership. It's a pose.[15]

In one other way, it is in the woman's own best interests to submit to her husband. Nothing causes a man to be more unloving and irresponsible than a wife who refuses to submit herself to his authority. The one thing most likely to make a man desire to wander is a woman who fails to give him love and respect. The truth is, far more men leave home in search of respect and esteem than in quest of sexual pleasure.

Conversely, few things will bring a man around quicker than a wife who can present her opinions to her husband, but then, in the right spirit, say, "But whatever you decide I will support." This in effect places the man in a position where, if things go wrong, there will be no one else to blame. Men don't like that. That is why many men abdicate their leadership responsibility to their wives. They face enough failure in the world without having to experience more at home. But the woman who accepts the authority her husband tries to hand her, or who manipulates events to her liking instead of yielding to her husband and trusting God for the outcome, is doing herself a great disservice. By doing so she may be pushing away the one person whose love she most desires.

Paul Vitz says that the command to wives to obey husbands "speaks here to the weakness particularly common in women to disregard the rules, and to the natural male concern with rules, with order." He says, "In the marriage setting, disobedience undermines the husband's capacity to maintain commitment; to disregard authority is to remove his function and destroy his ability to carry out his responsibilities."[16]

Though much is expected of the woman, more is expected of the man. That's the side of the story that's seldom stressed. Ephesians 5 continues with its counsel for the husband:

> Husbands, love your wives, just as Christ also loved the church and gave Himself up for her; that He might sanctify her, having cleansed her by the washing of water with the word, that He might present to Himself the church in all her

glory, having no spot or wrinkle on any such thing; but that she should be holy and blameless. (Eph. 5:25-27)

Many men in some way or other expect their wives to be door-mats for them. This passage says instead that a man is to lay down *his* life for his wife. If she is expected to submit to him as the Church does to Christ, how can God expect less than that a husband must relate to his wife as Christ relates to his Church? To follow Christ's example in this respect a man must love his wife and give himself for her, crucifying his selfishness for the sake of his wife. Why? So he can purify her and sanctify her and present her whole and blameless on the Day of Judgment. Christ's patience with his betrothed, the Church, is to that end: to teach us to please him and to enable us to overcome our defects and weaknesses that we might be his spotless bride at the marriage feast of the Lamb (Rev. 19:7).

Isn't this also contrary to the expectations society has? We usually think that the wild and restless young man just "needs a good woman" to settle him down and set him straight, but the biblical view is just the opposite. God doesn't expect a woman to be nursing a blubbering, immature little boy who refuses to grow up. It is God's intention that a man be mature enough to lead, strengthen, and nurture his family.

A real man isn't some pseudo-macho clod who proves his virility by running with the boys, drinking, gambling, and squandering away the food from his family's table. This is the childish, pitiable specimen that television-oriented society produces because it has lost a true sense of what it means to be a man after God's image. Unless we restore the Church to biblical principles of male-female relationships, we shall see more people turn in vain to such slovenly and inadequate means of authenticating their gender.

According to the Lord's plan for husbands, a real man in many cases can help his wife attain new levels of wholeness and self-actualization. Through sacrificial love he will help her recognize her worth and preciousness as a person in God's sight, and so free her to be the best possible person she can be – and the happiest!

Why should a man do this? Paul elaborates:

Even so husbands should love their wives as [being in a sense] their own bodies. He who loves his own wife loves him-

136

self. For no man ever hated his own flesh, but nourishes and carefully protects and cherishes it, as Christ does the church, because we are members (parts) of His body. For this reason a man shall leave his father and his mother and shall be joined to his wife, and the two shall become one flesh. This mystery is very great, but I speak concerning [the relation of] Christ and the church. (Eph. 5:28-32, AMP.)

The husband-wife relationship is to be modeled after Christ's relationship to the Church as its eternal Bridegroom. The teachings of Scriptures move directly against the grain of the world's natural inclinations. In our society there is an increasing tendency for marriage to be regarded as two remaining two; no effort is spared to see that one's own will is left inviolate. "You do your thing and I'll do mine. . . . " So the saying goes. "I won't ask too much of you because I really don't want you demanding too much of me." But are such marriages working, or are they merely being consumed by selfishness? Marriage shouldn't be a duel in the midst of a war. God's plan for the most intimate relationship on this earth far transcends that description.

Ephesians teaches that when a man and woman marry they are to become one after the pattern of Christ's union with us. Therein is the key to the man's ability to make the necessary sacrifices. What is taught here goes far beyond the oneness of sexual union. It reflects a basic union of wills and merging of purposes that can only be accomplished through God's love. When such a union takes place, the strife, willfulness, and discord that characterize many modern marriages are replaced with the harmony and tranquility that dwell wherever there is true caring.

You see, if two become one, then the man must realize that he can never actually advance his own well-being at the expense of his wife's. She is not just some autonomous and disjointed appendage, but rather the other half of his soul. Something will truly be good for him only if it is also good for his wife. Just as a man would not harm one part of his body in order to help another, so also will a sensible man not do anything contrary to his wife's well-being in some vain and misguided attempt to gratify his own selfishness. When a man and woman become one under God, each person's well-being is inevitably and inextricably linked to his or her partner. As Christ views each person in the Church as a part of his earthly body and labors to make sure all that happens will work for his good, so will the wise husband see to it that all decisions he makes are predicated on his wife's as well as his own welfare. Selfishness is counterproductive. It is foolish to rob one pocket to fill the other. Such a way of relating can never lead to happiness.

It is obvious that when a man and woman pledge themselves to truly care for one another, their love and respect for each other will grow. Their marriage will be a school of love as well as of sacrifice – a place where the nurturance, support, and caring for each other's needs can be provided. The home can become a place where true growth as people made in the image of God can take place.

Marriage can be an oasis of love and affirmation in a desert of greed and rejection. When this happens the Christian family can be a radical witness to a loveless world. A good marriage *is* the best school of theology. In today's society when such a marriage is indeed a rare and precious sight, it can become a glorious reflection of the God who is love, showing the difference that the eternal Bridegroom makes in our lives.

A good Christian marriage is the key to the fulfillment of the marriage partners. Far from obliterating each partner's distinct personalities, a good marriage creates a secure environment for people to become all that the Lord created them to be. Because both men and women need love and respect, above all else, Paul ends Ephesians 5 in this way:

> Let each man of you (without exception) love his wife as [being in a sense] his very own self; and let the wife see that she respects and reverences her husband – that she notices him, regards him, honors him, prefers him, venerates and esteems him; and that she defers to him, praises him, and loves and admires him exceedingly. (v. 33, AMP.)

Wise is the woman who understands the male temperament sufficiently to crucify her inclinations to nag, complain, and condemn (Prov. 14:1; 19:13; 21:9; 27:15). When she reacts instead with understanding and loving reverence and sees the good in her mate, she will be well on the way to learning how God can make her husband the man to whom she always wanted to be married.

Wiser still is the man who learns to love his wife in a sacrificial way. Ultimately this is the most rewarding way to live, for everything he pours into her will be returned with interest. Truly, as the text of the wedding ceremony says, any couple who will "stead- fastly endeavor to do the will of (their) heavenly Father" will have a life that is "full of joy, and the home which (they) are establishing will abide in peace."[17]

THIRTEEN
SPIRITUAL AUTHORITY
AND SOCIAL RENEWAL

This relationship of the persons in the Trinity models a biblically authentic way to relate to authority. If we can learn the lessons which the godhead and biblical sexual differences have to teach us about the true nature of authority, we will go a long way toward solving one of society's major problems: the lack of proper leadership. In its stead we find the perversion and misuse of authority and the destructive exertion of human willfulness that is the root of so many of our social, interpersonal, and international problems.

The problems our society has with authority are legion, yet without a just exercise of authority, no civilization can long endure. As Bob Mumford says:

> We have been predisposed against all authority figures by our society and especially by the media. Television fathers are overgrown infants who are mothered by their wives, corrected by their children, and who don't have enough brains to take their vitamins. Presidents are pictured as mindless and petty; law enforcement officers as corrupt; parents as cruel and unreliable; preachers as effeminate and immoral; all political leaders as con men. Our heroes are the law breakers, the criminals, the goldbricks or the guys who beat the system. Is it any wonder we have difficulty teaching our children respect for authority or that we have difficulty saying, "Blessed is he that comes in the name of the Lord?"[1]

Probably the reason we have such a hard time with authority is that most of our leaders, even in the Church, have never learned to exercise authority biblically. Attempts to use "inclusive language" to somehow neuter our understanding of God reflect this. We want an egalitarian God – one who has little real authority in our lives. By giving him other titles, we can make him after our image rather than conform to his.

Jesus solved our authority problem differently. He came to teach us a whole new approach to authority. However, it is one that unfortunately has been largely forgotten in our generation. He said:

> The kings of the Gentiles lord it over them [their subjects]; and those who have authority over them are called "Benefactors." But not so with you, but let him who is the greatest among you become as the youngest, and the leader as the servant. For who is greater, the one who reclines at table, or the one who serves? Is it not the one who reclines at table? But I am among you as the one who serves. (Luke 22:25-27)

Jesus, the Lord of Hosts and King of Kings, came to earth to serve his heavenly Father. He served his Father in heaven by serving the men whom God had given to him on earth; he served them by giving them righteous, exemplary leadership. He taught them how to live. He also taught his followers that if they would learn to serve as he had, it would be a source of great blessing for them.

Husbands and wives must similarly learn these lessons. It is essential to the divine plan for marriage. Husbands are commanded to "live with your wives in an understanding way, as with a weaker vessel, since she is a woman; and grant her honor as a fellow heir of the grace of life so that your prayers may not be hindered" (1 Pet. 3:7). In doing this a man will be following the example of the Church's heavenly husband.

Those who would quote the Apostle Paul's injunction that in Christ there is no male nor female and neglect to understand what he meant by that are not doing women, men, the Church, or our world any favors. Such abuse of a text with context is a deceptive pretext, and a destructive one at that. The same Paul who penned those words taught clear role distinctions as we've seen in Ephesians 5 and elsewhere. Because a woman is an equal heir of God's grace, this does not make her equal in roles and authority to her husband. She is called to be in submission to her husband, doing what is right without being frightened by any fear. This certainly does not make her any more inferior than Jesus is to God, though his earthly will was in all ways submitted to the Father's.

The godly husband's job, though it wouldn't seem so at first, is at least as difficult as the wife's. It requires a greater exercise of serving leadership. He is to "rule his household well." Christ is the head of every man and the man is the head of his wife and family. (As the husband will often need his Lord's understanding for his shortcomings and weaknesses, so also will the wife often need her husband's understanding.) However, God the Father is not the ultimate permissive parent. His compassion towards his children who fear him properly (a proper fear of God is awareness of the consequences of disobedience) never motivates him to rescind his righteous commandments. His understanding of our weaknesses never leads him to tolerate our disobedience. The Lord knows we are clay; he made us that way. But he also knows it's in our best interests to obey him. His strength can compensate for our weaknesses and enable us to live on a higher plane than we could otherwise attain without him.

It is the nature of a righteous Father's love to call us to that higher plane; to stretch us beyond our natural inclinations. A godly father and husband is charged with the obligation to rule well: to help his wife learn to "be his glory," and to train his children up in the nurture and admonition of the Lord. It is easier for a wife to drop the kids at the day care center and hold down a regular job than it is to become all that a godly wife and mother should be. So also it is far easier for a man to abrogate his responsibility to rule and lose himself in bringing home the bacon. Accepting responsibility is as contrary to the nature of most men as submission is to most women. But many of the problems of our society will never be solved as long as we continue to take the easier way. As J. Edgar Hoover once said, "There is but one way to eliminate juvenile delinquency," (and I would add unwanted pregnancies, abortions, homosexuality, venereal disease, divorce, and the vast toll of human suffering these problems cause) "that is by providing each child in America with competent parents." As Charles Simpson says, social problems are family problems that never got solved.

Similarly there is but one way to eliminate the widespread disenchantment with marriage and relationships: provide each woman in America with competent husbands. What is it women want? We ought better to ask what they need. They don't need macho maniacs or detached wimps. They need husbands who are willing to learn the lessons of authority modeled for us by the persons in the Godhead. As the Father taught the Son to do only that which pleased the Father, and the Spirit sought never his own glory but only the Son's, so also ought men to righteously rule their families. Christian men must teach our wives the joy of serving God through honoring their husband's headship. Only then can husband and wife learn to train their children to honor their parents and thus be protected from many evil and unwise decisions in life.

Men should be learning this serving leadership at home before they are given authority in the Church. One of the major problems in many churches today is that their ruling boards are filled with people who've never met the biblical criterion for exercising mature spiritual leadership. Only the man who rules his household well is properly equipped to exercise authority in the Church.

The Church, through training its members in the proper exercise of and relationships to authority in the home, could have been preparing them for providing biblical leadership in society. Instead, we've somehow considered those lessons too difficult and opted for what appeared in the short run to be an easier way. Ironically, shamefully, in many instances today the deceived modern church is leading the rebellion against biblical authority and role relationships. All of society is suffering proportionately from the feminization of leadership.

All of this has more to do with sexual satisfaction than may first meet the eye. It will be impossible for a woman to derive fulfillment from her relationship with a man whose leadership she has emasculated. It is equally unlikely that a man will be able to enjoy more than momentary pleasure from his wife when he has been emotionally distant from her and refused to accept his responsibility to lead and understand her in her weaknesses.

The God who created us male and female after his image has much to teach about true satisfaction. Only he who loses his life will save (satisfy, fulfill, and make whole) his life. Only he who learns to serve as Jesus served will discover the secrets of abundant life which Jesus came to give us. We don't need more power, pride, and prestige. The world has already suffered enough abuse at the hands of those who've worshiped these unworthy idols. Rather we must embrace the humility and serving leadership so perfectly exemplified for us in the life of Jesus and the interrelationships of the persons in the godhead. Only then will we find rest for our souls. Only then can we provide the world with leadership that solves rather than compounds its multitudinous problems.

The deference modeled for us by the persons in the godhead can show us the way to a saner society. We need the Comforter that the Holy Spirit is. We also need the principled Truth that Jesus is. We must learn to submit our lives to the glory of God the Father as both the Son and the Spirit do. If we properly apply these lessons from our heavenly family, our earthly family and the Church can become concrete models of the kingdom come to earth. If we adopt a defective pattern for our families, churches, and society and distort or pervert these most significant relationships, we will only lead the world into deeper chaos and confusion.

The blueprint always decides the shape of the dwelling place. May we clearly discern the eternal wisdom subtly concealed in the Trinity and may we graciously shape our lives to its higher call and glory.

FOURTEEN
BROKEN COVENANTS, BROKEN PEOPLE: THE QUESTION OF DIVORCE AND REMARRIAGE

Having been raised in a very liberal, mainline Protestant congregation, I was quite convinced that the Roman Catholic church's strict posture on divorce was mercilessly unrighteous. A liberated attitude toward divorce in the late fifties and early sixties was to mainline Protestantism what the acceptance of abortion-on-demand was in the seventies and homosexuality is in the eighties. Many, like myself, considered divorce to be a compassionate expression of God's mercy. Few anticipated the tidal wave of irresponsibility that developed, leaving in its wake virtually millions of neglected wives and children, and spawning myriad social problems such as battered wives, single-parent households, sexual abuse, rape, and incest.

I had been so indoctrinated with humanistic values concerning divorce that immediately after my conversion, when I first took the Bible seriously, I was astonished at the gravity of Jesus' perspective on it. It was a rude awakening to learn that the Catholics were much closer to the truth than we "enlightened" Protestants were.

Until that time, I had been totally taken in by the inversion of truth in contemporary religion, the liberal tendency to confuse the clean with the unclean (Isa. 32:5; Prov. 17:15). In this area, as in many others today, the religious community has exchanged the truth of God for a lie (Rom. 1:25). They have adopted a new, allegedly higher ethical standard that has led to the acceptance of sin

147

and the rejection of scriptural righteousness.

While the perversion of values in this area has caused much harm to multitudes of individuals and to society as a whole, we must avoid an equally unbalanced overreaction on divorce and remarriage. The Scriptures, rightly understood, present a clear and balanced perspective on divorce. The Bible's position on the subject is rooted in the character of the God in whose image we have been created. Its wisdom is founded upon his infinite fore-knowledge of the unavoidable consequences of disobedience or deviation from his norms. It is presented with our highest good in mind.

DIVORCE IN THE OLD TESTAMENT

In the Old Testament, under Moses' law, a man could divorce his wife for certain specifically stipulated reasons (Deut. 24:1-4). The wife was privileged to marry again. However, if her second husband divorced her, the first husband was forbidden to remarry her (Jer. 3:1). These laws were greatly abused, eventually leading the Lord to say he hated divorce (Mal. 2:16). He hated it, first of all, because as our heavenly Husband (Isa. 62:4-5), he would never leave nor forsake us (Heb. 13:5). He would never violate his part of his covenant with us. He also hated divorce because he loves people. He knows the harm divorce inflicts upon the human psyche.

Too often those who have held to a high view of marriage and its permanence have led people to believe that God's hatred of divorce is also a hatred of those divorced. This is unfortunate and could not be farther from the truth. God hates divorce because he loves the people whom it devastates and hates to see them suffer the savage wrenching of their souls.

Perhaps we can better understand the Lord's hatred of divorce by examining what it does to us. The word *sex* is based on the word *secare*, meaning to cut or divide. When the Lord took Eve from Adam's rib (Gen. 2:21-24), he divided woman from man, thus making it impossible for either to be perfectly whole without the other (1 Cor. 11:8-12). In a biblical marriage, the Lord rejoins woman to man. Their union enables them to achieve a completion that would otherwise be impossible for either to attain alone. Because we were made male and female after God's image, the proper relating of each sex to the other is necessary to fully reflect the Creator's glory.

The marriage covenant is the Lord's instrument for achieving that reunion. Through it he enables the two to become one (Matt. 19:5). In fact, the very nature of the marriage covenant is to bind together two beings who would otherwise be separate.[1]

Jesus recognized the oneness of a husband and wife and its significance as to the question of divorce. He mentioned it in the Gospel of Mark when the Pharisees cross-examined him on the subject. In answer to their queries, he asked them what Moses commanded:

> And they said, "Moses permitted a man to write a certificate of divorce and send her away." But Jesus said to them, "Because of your hardness of heart he wrote you this commandment. But from the beginning of creation, God made them male and female. For this cause a man shall leave his father and mother, and the two shall become one flesh; consequently they are no longer two, but one flesh. What therefore God has joined together, let no man separate." (Mark 10:4-9)

We are commanded not to separate what God has joined together because the two have become one. When two pieces of wood are cemented together properly, any force seeking to pull them apart would probably split the wood before it wrecks their bond, thus leaving at least one piece of the wood shattered and broken.

Divorce does a similar thing to people. When the Lord joins them together, they become one. That which seeks to break their bond would, in the process, break one or both of them instead. This tearing apart of the two who have become one leaves scars on the soul that are almost impossible to heal. Of course, the damage done to the children who are a product of that union, and the ultimate effect that these hurting and broken lives have on society, are equally permanent and destructive.

DIVORCE IN THE NEW TESTAMENT

After Jesus gave this teaching, the disciples questioned him privately about the ramifications of his position on divorce. He said to them, "Whoever divorces his wife and marries another woman commits adultery against her; and if she herself divorces her husband and marries another man, she is committing adultery" (Mark 10:11-12). This statement is remarkably serious in light of the fact that unrepented adultery excludes a person from God's kingdom (1 Cor. 6:9-10).

This passage taken out of context and isolated from the rest of Scripture appears to forbid all remarriage by divorced persons. There is no question of the fact that Jesus stressed the sanctity of marriage and the seriousness of divorce and adultery.

One text alone, however, does not complete the revelation of God on the subject. Jesus gives a brief incidental reply to a question posed to him by the disciples. But it is obvious, from other passages in the Bible, that God had more to say on the subject. Jesus' response, important though it is, does not exhaust the topic.

The great theologian and Bible teacher E. J. Carnell said that in interpreting the Bible, didactic (teaching) passages should be used to interpret incidental ones. It is also a commonly accepted principle of interpretation to allow later expositions of a subject to elaborate on the implications of earlier ones. Both Jesus and the Apostle Paul made later statements on divorce that need to be consulted as we investigate the appropriateness or permissibility of remarriage. As we turn our attention to those passages, it becomes clear that there are times when remarriage after a divorce is biblically permissible.

One such passage that we must examine is Jesus' statement on divorce in the Sermon on the Mount. In this context Jesus is speaking about adultery (Matt. 5:27-32). He contrasts his position to the permissiveness of Moses and Jeremiah (Deut. 24:1-3; Jer. 3:1): "It was said, 'Whoever sends his wife away, let him give her a certificate of divorce'; but I say to you that everyone who divorces his wife, except for the cause of unchastity, makes her commit adultery; and whoever marries a divorced woman commits adultery" (Matt. 5:31-32).

The seriousness of adultery is underscored by the preceding verses, which first establish the fact that he who lusts after a woman in his heart is an adulterer (vv. 27-28). Second, it is affirmed by Jesus' prescription for such sins: tear out the offending eye, amputate the uncontrolled hand. It would be better to enter heaven maimed than to burn in hell whole (vv. 29-30). But what of the condition "except for the cause of unchastity"? Because of the consequences of misleading people through an improper interpretation of this passage, it is essential that we accurately understand what this exception clause means.

Matthew Henry, the great Puritan commentator, says of this text that "divorce is not to be allowed, except in the case of adultery, which breaks the marriage covenant."[2] The word here translated as adultery *(unchastity* in the New American Standard Bible) is πορνείας *(porneias)*, or *fornication*. It comes from the Greek word πόρνη, a derivative of the verb πέρνημι, "to sell." It refers especially to slaves, meaning literally "harlot for hire or prostitute."[3] It refers to all manner of illicit sexual intercourse.

This same word is used later in the Gospel of Matthew, when Jesus is asked why Moses allowed a husband to put away his wife with a certificate of divorce. He said it was "because of your hardness of heart . . . ; but from the beginning it has not been this way. And I say to you, whoever divorces his wife, except for immorality, and marries another commits adultery *[πορνείχ]"* (Matt. 19:8-9).

These exception clauses do not appear in Mark or Luke. This is all the more significant because Matthew's uncompromising Jewish exposition "usually tends to a stronger view of the Torah, whereas this is a notable divergence."[4] This Matthean text is probably original, perhaps predating Luke and Mark. It certainly is not open to challenge on textual grounds.

What is Jesus saying to us in these passages? Through Matthew, he is

> telling his Jewish Christian readers that if a man puts away his wife except for her infidelity, in which case he is compelled to do so by existing statutes, he is driving her into an adulterous relation should she remarry. . . . The drift of the clause, then, is not that the Christian husband, should his wife be unfaithful, is permitted to divorce her, but that if he is legally forced to do this he should not be open to criticism if by her conduct his wife has made the continuation of the marriage quite impossible.[5]

What of us today who feel we are not bound by the strict Jewish legalisms of Jesus' day? It was to those situations, I believe, that the Apostle Paul was speaking in 1 Corinthians 7. In a clearly didactic passage dealing extensively with issues related to marriage and divorce he says:

> But I say to the unmarried and to widows that it is good for them if they remain even as I. But if they do not have self-control, let them marry; for it is better to marry than to burn [with passion]. But to the married I give instructions, not I, but the Lord, that the wife should not leave her husband (but if she does leave, let her remain unmarried, or else be reconciled to her husband), and that the husband should not send his wife away [or depart from her]. But to the rest I say, not the Lord, that if any brother has a wife who is an unbeliever, and she consents to live with him, let him not send her away. And a woman who has an unbelieving husband, and he consents to live with her, let her not send her husband away. For the unbelieving husband is sanctified through his wife, and the unbelieving wife is sanctified through her believing husband; for otherwise your children are unclean, but now they are holy. Yet if the unbelieving one leaves, let him leave; the brother or the sister is not under bondage in such cases, but God has called us to peace. For how do you know, O wife, whether you will save your husband? Or how do you know, O husband, whether you will save your wife? Only, as the Lord has assigned to each one, as God has called each, in this manner let him walk. And thus I direct in all the churches. (vv. 8-17)

THE QUESTION OF REMARRIAGE

This passage became very real to me when I was in seminary and was asked to perform my first marriage. Previously I had read *The Christian Family* by Larry Christenson. In it he quotes Martin Luther's statement:

> Where they are not Christians, or perverse and false Christians, it would be well for the authorities to allow them, like heathens, to put away their wives, and to take others, in order that they may not, with their discordant lives, have two hells, both here and there. But let them know that by their divorce

they cease to be Christians, and become heathens, and are in a state of damnation.[6]

In light of that remarkably strong statement, I believed all remarriage to be forbidden for any Christian in all instances. Then a close friend came seeking my counsel. He felt the Lord wanted him to marry a young woman who had met the Lord in our coffeehouse. The only problem was that she was divorced!

You can imagine my personal turmoil. I had to indisputably resolve the issue of divorce and remarriage. I could not mislead them. I asked them to postpone their marriage, pending my resolution of the matter.

For three months I read everything I could find on the subject and picked the brains of each of my professors. I discovered a multitude of diverse and conflicting counsel among Bible-believing Christians. Some taught that if the marriage were performed in their church, God's blessing would be upon it. Therefore, divorce and remarriage in "the true church" were permissible. Other pastors would not perform a marriage for divorced people, but if a couple could find someone else to marry them, they would later be welcomed into the membership of the "pure" church. When I was a United Methodist pastor I grew weary of having couples thus referred to me by other pastors. One person told me that adultery was forgivable; the first act of intercourse in remarriage was a sin for which the couple needed to ask forgiveness, but they were then free to be legitimately married.

Finally I concluded that the matter could be resolved only through a careful examination of Scripture. I gave my young friends a list of the relevant passages and attacked the same list myself, carefully dissecting each phrase. I knew that if I consented to marry them, they would also need to study these passages before they were married, or these verses might haunt them long after their wedding.

The passage in 1 Corinthians 7 and a related passage in Romans 7 gave me the light I needed. I saw that if an unbelieving mate departed, as was the case in my friend's previous marriage, the believer was not required to coerce his or her partner back into their covenant relationship. She was to let him leave that peace might reign in her home. It goes without saying that this does not give a Christian the right to drive away a stubborn or unbelieving partner, nor should a Christian ever divorce a believing mate. If this does happen, remarriage is out of the question. But I still needed to know if remarriage was permissible for my friend in the wake of her unbelieving mate's departure.

As I was meditating on the meaning of the passage, "If the unbelieving one leaves, let him leave; the brother or the sister is not under bondage in such cases" (1 Cor. 7:15), the word *bondage* stood out. The passage in Romans 7 came to mind. I quickly flipped to it. Here Paul speaks of the fact that the law has jurisdiction over a person as long as they are alive. He says:

> For the married woman is bound by law to her husband while he is living; but if her husband dies, she is released from the law concerning the husband. So then if, while her husband is living, she is joined to another man, she shall be called an adulteress; but if her husband dies, she is free from the law, so that she is not an adulteress, though she is joined to another man. (vv. 2-3)

Paul uses this passage to illustrate the way in which believers who are dead to the law can be joined to Christ. He says they "have been released from the law, having died to that by which we were *bound [κατειχόμεθα]*, so that we serve in newness of the Spirit and not in oldness of the letter" (v. 6).

Two words are used in Romans 7 for being bound to a marriage relationship. The first, *δέδεται (dedetai)*, in verse 2 means "to bind together" or "supernatural binding" and "can be used of the mutual commitment of partners in marriage," as it is used here and in 1 Corinthians 7:27 and 39.[7] The second is similar but even stronger. It is the verb *δουλεύειν (dooloain)* meaning "held fast so as to serve." It is derived from the noun *δοῦλος (doolos)* which means "slave," causing "absolute subjection of the total loss of autonomy."[8] It is the same word used in 1 Corinthians 7:15 to express "total binding by another." Such a person who is so enslaved "is prepared to forego personal rights."[9]

I saw that since the word used for the marriage bond in Romans 7 is the same as the word used for being loosed from that bond in 1 Corinthians 7, remarriage is sometimes permissible. In Romans 7 the freedom to remarry occurs in the event of the partner's death. In 1 Corinthians 7 the believer is similarly loosed from that bond if the unbeliever departs and refuses reconciliation. Scripture speaks of unbelievers as being *dead* in their trespasses and sins (Col. 2:13; Eph. 2:1, 5), not dying. If, in God's eyes, they are indeed dead, then a believer is free to remarry.

I urge great caution here. Since an unbelieving mate can be "sanctified" by the believing partner (1 Cor. 7:14), all efforts toward reconciliation must be pursued. The believer must do all in his or her power to relate to the unbelieving mate in a manner that would make that person desire salvation (Acts 16:31; 1 Pet. 3:1-8; 1 Cor. 7:12-17).

However, once it is clear that the unbeliever has departed and will be reconciled neither to God nor to the believing mate, the brother or sister is no longer bound to that marriage vow. If sexual continence is difficult, one would be better off married to a believer than burning in lust and living promiscuously, blaspheming the Lord (1 Cor. 7:8-9). Young widows are encouraged to remarry and bear children (1 Tim. 5:14-15), and anyone who does not have the gift of celibacy should also marry (Matt. 19:9-12).

As I prayed over all of this and how to relate it to the friends who desired to marry, I felt I still needed more confirmation. Since I believe that the Lord has a specific, perfect will for each of his people and that they are best fulfilled by discovering it, I needed to know more than the biblical principles that were related to their situation. I needed to know if it was the Lord's perfect will for them to be married to one another.

Once I felt free to consider their remarriage, the Lord brought to my mind the three-year-old daughter of the young woman's first marriage. "Do you love her?" the Lord seemed to be asking me. "Yes, Lord," I said. "Am I a God of great mercy and compassion?" "Of course," I replied. I then had my answer. Our heavenly Father well understands the need for a father in the life of every child. I sensed he was telling me that he would indeed desire and bless their union. I later discovered that many Bible-believing Christians believe that a person who is divorced before giving his or her life to the Lord, like my friend, is free to remarry.

After ascertaining that the young man and his fiancée were willing not to marry if it wasn't God's best for them, I consented to marry them. It was my first marriage as a young pastor. Strange, in light of the fact that I had once believed very strongly that divorced people should never remarry. That couple has served the

Lord together faithfully now for over ten years. They have two other children, and their home and family has been a haven of rest and sanctuary to many single people over the years. They seem to have a unique call to counsel, support, and guide people with troubled marriages.

I realize that what I am saying here about the possibilities of remarriage can and will be construed by some as a carte blanche endorsement of irresponsible divorce. That indeed would be unfortunate. Every marriage is important to God. Every effort should be taken to encourage reconciliation whenever possible. No remarriage should be performed where the possibility for reconciliation exists. This is especially true in the case of two believers. A serious attempt should be made to bring the one who has separated from his or her mate to repentance and reconciliation because a believer who leaves his spouse transgresses a moral absolute and is "dead while he lives" (1 Cor. 6:9-10) if he seeks to be joined to another.

When it is clear that reconciliation is impossible, remarriage for the offended believing mate is a possibility. The same pastoral care and supervision should be exercised here as they would be in any anticipated marriage to ascertain the clear and perfect will of God for the couple. No marriage ever should be performed on the rebound, nor should it occur if the couple is unwilling to consider not being married. People who are unwilling to receive pastoral direction in such a crucial area, wanting their own will more than the Lord's, probably won't be able to make a marriage work.

Extensive premarital counseling must be required of both. I require a minimum of six sessions in which I use an excellent handbook that explores Scriptures related to sex, finances, sex roles, in-laws, vacations, communication, and other subjects.[10] I may require more than six sessions if I sense it is needed. This is especially true in cases of remarriage, where inner wounds and hurts may need to be healed in order for the relationship to succeed.

THE CHURCH AND MARRIAGE

It is time for us to acknowledge that churches are largely to blame for the failure of many marriages in our generation. I believe we would not have the millions of divorces or the spiritual and emotional hurt that has been left in their wake if the mainline Protestant churches had not departed from biblical standards. On top of that, congregations have kept pastors too busy with bureaucracy and other nonpastoral obligations to pastor as they ought. Clergy have not taught as faithfully as they should what the Bible clearly says about Christ's lordship, marriage, sex, sexual roles, or the seriousness of divorce. Their own marriages have seldom been exemplary. They have rarely counseled teens, engaged couples, troubled marrieds, or divorced people from a true biblical perspective.

People in the churches have not been sufficiently committed to the Lord, to their own young people, or to troubled persons in their midst to enable the church to be a "light on the hill" – God's instrument of reconciliation and healing. Clearly, there is much room for repentance, and we must remember that God's judgment begins in his own house (1 Pet. 4:17).

I believe the Church can change and so make a significant difference in our world. If we will repent, we can yet build families that can transform our culture. As someone once said, it is not the Church's job to create a new society. It is the Church's job to build the people who will create a new society. It is time for us to be about the task.

THE CRUX OF THE MATTER

Today, as in the days before Christ, the hardness of people's hearts causes divorce. And more often the problem is not with the other person. It is our own unwillingness to relinquish our rights and die to our own desires. Getting rid of one mate and finding another does not solve the problem, it only compounds it.

Secular psychology knows very little about this. Hence, when we listen to radio call-in counseling sessions, it seems the "experts" prescribe divorce in at least 50 percent of the calls they receive. Because such people usually know nothing of the security of a relationship with a covenant God, they have no capacity to honor their own covenants. (It seems most of these counselors are themselves divorced.) Consequently they can hardly encourage others to be faithful in tough situations.

Further reason for the promiscuous proliferation of divorces, however, stems from the fact that the secular world is largely powerless to enable people to endure marital struggles. Without the energizing power of God's Spirit, and apart from the wellspring of his all-merciful love, it is impossible to love as sacrificially as is necessary in a troubled marriage relationship. Only he who laid down his life for us, his earthly bride, can empower us to do the same for our beloved – and nothing less can ultimately succeed.

The pity in all of this is that if a couple work through the inevitable stresses and strains that seek to destroy their relationship, they can come out of those hard times better, more blessed, freed from the tyranny of their own selfishness, and with a deeper, more humble love for their mate. If they flee the relationship or refuse to handle their conflicts constructively, their lives will go downhill.

Properly handled, marital problems can be a source of interpersonal growth toward wholeness and bring people closer to God. Easy access to divorce short-circuits that growth. It consigns many people to a living hell, eternally locked within the prison of their own unmitigated selfishness. Truly it is God's love for us that causes him to mandate the permanence of marriage. It is his Spirit that infuses us with the power to fulfill that mandate, and his grace that enables us to do so joyfully to his glory.

FIFTEEN
THE HORSE WITHOUT
THE CARRIAGE:
WHAT'S WRONG WITH
PREMARITAL SEX

Like many of today's youth I was a teenager who saw nothing wrong with premarital sex. My parents were never comfortable enough to talk with me about the subject. My elementary school sex education course taught me everything I wanted to know about sex, except whether or not to engage in it. By the time I got to high school, my peers, the secular values of my sophisticated teachers, exposure to the *playboy* philosophy, and the embarrassed silence of my church all led me to conclude that premarital sex was a legitimate option; one that God would understand and condone. Certainly, I reasoned, he would not want me to be frustrated by repressing my sexual urges. As long as I loved someone, I was sure that sex with her was OK.

Ironically, however, the first girl with whom I was intimate I did not love at all. In fact, I sometimes wonder if I really loved any of the girls who followed. I do know that after years of sexual experimentation my whole life came crumbling down. I am convinced that the psychotic breakdown I experienced in college was largely due to unresolved guilt from years of premarital sexual activity. Now, as I look at what happened – and what might have happened – in my life, it is hard to believe that no one tried to warn me about the potential dangers of premarital sexual experimentation. Engaging in it, as the following statistics show, damages the lives of countless thousands of young people today and causes many millions more to suffer intensely. At best, widespread ignorance about premarital sex robs multitudes of a happy and fulfilling sex life.

159

IS SEX EDUCATION WORKING?

Though there is more sex education than ever before, there are also more sex-related problems. A 1980 survey by Drs. Melvin Zelnik and John Kanter of the Johns Hopkins School of Public Health reported that almost half of all teenage women in U.S. metropolitan areas were sexually active. This was up from 30.4 percent in 1971. By 1986 half of all girls seventeen and under had had sexual intercourse. The average age of first intercourse among teenage girls was 16.2 years. More than a quarter of these sexually active teens never used contraception. Of these young women, about two-thirds became pregnant.[1] Astonishingly, those who use contraceptives are 20 percent more likely to become pregnant unintentionally than girls who do not use contraception.[2] That is why it is so hard to understand the twisted logic of Planned Parenthood groups that are trying to put birth control clinics in high schools as a solution for teen pregnancies. Putting it another way, probably "4 of every 10 girls aged fourteen will become pregnant at least once during their teen-age years, 2 of 10 would give birth and more than 1 in 7 would have an abortion."[3]

Birth statistics confirm these research findings. Twenty-one percent of all births in the United States occur in the age group between twelve and nineteen; half of these girls are unmarried. Even with the widespread acceptance of abortion, births by teenage girls have increased by 33 percent within the past five years. Half of the more than 500,000 teenage pregnancies annually end in abortion.[4] Most of these are performed without parental consultation. (Though a consent form must be signed for a girl to get her ears pierced, it is illegal to inform parents if their child seeks an abortion.)

DOESN'T THE CHURCH HELP?

Suprisingly, that nice young person you see in church with his or her parents is likely to be as sexually active as the teenager who does not go to church. A recent survey on teenage sexuality in the United Methodist Church disclosed some surprising findings. Fewer than half of the thirteen- to fifteen-year-old boys and 78 percent of the girls surveyed think premarital sex is "wrong according to the Christian faith." Even fewer of the sixteen- to eighteen-year-olds felt that way.[5] Why is this happening to our church kids? As my friend Terry Hallock of Family Alert says, "We give children 'rights' but no philosophy of life upon which to base the use of these rights. This is the good life?" he wisely asks.

IS THIS THE GOOD LIFE?

What is the good life? Is it the fact that two thousand young girls get pregnant every Saturday night?[6] This shouldn't surprise us. In our quest for the good life we have made education an idol, demanding that our children postpone marriage often until their mid-twenties. We've bombarded them with movies, sitcoms, records, and even required reading in high school literature courses that make them feel strange if they don't condone premarital sex and haven't engaged in it by age sixteen. Kids today are immoral for the same reason their parents were moral: they think society expects it of them.

The absentee father further aggravates the problem. Men have been so absent from the families that their wives may as well be widows; we have raised a whole generation of children who may as well be orphans, though their parents are still living. Our incredible divorce rate and the influence of the women's movement have combined to produce a pitiful generation of latchkey kids who think sex might help them find the kind of love they never had at home. As a consequence, many young girls today think that a baby will provide them with the unconditional love that neither Mom nor Dad had the time to give them. Many young boys, in the absence of positive male role models, are turning to sexual conquests, or ironically, homosexual encounters, as a way of proving their virility, attractiveness, and worth.

"HELP ME UNDERSTAND . . ."

If we expect people to live moral lives, we need to help them understand why they should. God is not a celestial killjoy. He invented sex, and he chose to make it pleasurable. He forbids sex only in settings that could harm us. His Word is given to help us find the context in which sex can be a blessing to us. Though the Bible has much sound counsel on premarital sex, unfortunately most people are ignorant of its advice.

Before I knew much about the Bible, I thought it condemned only adultery. I thought sex before marriage was OK in God's eyes. After my conversion I was surprised to learn that the Bible also condemned fornication (premarital sex—1 Cor. 6:9-10). Since God warns us in order to help us avoid harmful things, he must have good reasons for cautioning us to avoid premarital sex. What are they?

Reason 1. The world's view of sexuality is based on a fundamental misunderstanding of human nature. We have already examined (in chapter 5) the deficiencies in Freud's philosophies of sexuality. Unrestrained sexuality leads to bondage, not freedom and fulfillment. Love is more important than sex. In fact, love can be mortally wounded by irresponsible sexuality. Guilt is real, not just psychological. If we ignore guilt's early warning signals, we can harden our hearts to its judgments, but in so doing we also harden our hearts to the possibility of love and tenderness. Our greatest needs are not physical. All these factors and the others we discussed are crucial to the discussion of premarital sex. Spirituality, not sensuality, is the key to our total well-being and fulfillment.

Sex without love is as satisfying as a sneeze. This illustrates much of our frustration and emptiness in the age of so-called liberation. Only sex in the context of a totally committed, permanent, loving relationship is capable of fulfilling us. That is the first reason why God warns us to avoid premarital sex. Sex without love cannot make us happy. It can't fill our inner emptiness. Instead, it extinguishes the love we so desperately need.

Reason 2. The probability of an unwanted pregnancy. In college I almost committed suicide when I thought my girlfriend was pregnant. I wonder how many teenage suicides today are related to the fear of an unwanted pregnancy. In one area of the United States 13,000 girls under fourteen delivered babies in the same year.[7] Forty percent of the girls who turn fourteen this year are expected to become pregnant while they are still teenagers.[8] Many abortions are forced on these girls against their own moral judgment by uninformed parents who care more about their own reputation than they do about the health of their own daughter or grandchild.

For a class project, one high school teacher requires every student to carry a chicken egg in a box around school for a certain period of time. This experience gives each student a tiny hint of what it is like to be totally responsible for the well-being of another. This is a provocative educational simulation, highly appropriate in our age of manifold unwanted pregnancies and abortions.

Every teenager and young adult needs to ask himself or herself if sex is worth the risk. Other questions worth asking: What would it be like to have a baby now? How about an abortion? God never intended for us to face such awful choices alone. That's another reason why he warns us to avoid fornication. Every teenager should think about that this weekend, unless he or she wants to join the ranks of the other four thousand young people last weekend who thought, for one reason or another, that it couldn't happen to them. The best contraceptive is still "No!"

Reason 3. The threat of venereal disease. The alarming rise of venereal disease in America was highlighted on a Phil Donahue television program. It was revealed that new cases of gonorrhea rose from about 240,000 in 1959 to 500,000 in 1969 to more than one million in 1979. That's an increase of more than 400 percent in twenty years. Syphilis during that same period rose from 9,000 new cases in 1959 to more than 24,000 in 1979. Of course these statistics reflect reported cases only. Far more go unreported. Current studies on venereal disease tell us that "next to the common cold, gonorrhea is the second most common disease in the United States. Every fifteen seconds, night and day, someone gets a case of it."[9] More frightening is the incredible increase in oral and genital herpes. There is no cure for common strains of this disease. Herpes is harder to document because records are not required for those who seek treatment. It is estimated that there are 3 to 8 million cases of venereal herpes annually. Twenty to 30 percent of the sexually active population may already have been infected by it, and many don't know that they have.

Herpes is a disease that can recur from one to twelve or more times a year. It totally reorients one's life and future, causing intense emotional and physical pain. It can keep a person from marrying, can kill a baby who becomes infected by it (the mortality rate for infected newborns is 60 percent), and, so far, it has never been cured. In addition, those who contract herpes face an increased risk of cancer and a lifetime of physical torment.[10]

The AIDS virus, which is virtually always associated with

homosexuals, is showing up increasingly in heterosexual relationships. *Newsweek* magazine recently reported the tragic story of a young woman whose husband, an intravenous drug user, had divorced her years earlier and then died of AIDS. Though she had not had intercourse with him for a number of years, the virus lay dormant, surfacing and taking her life years later.[11] One casual affair with an AIDS carrier can lead to death many years down the road. Is premarital sex worth dying for?

Other forms of venereal disease also can infect innocent children or surface years later, causing blindness, nerve disorders, and even insanity. Few who have contracted a venereal disease ever thought they would get it, but there is no foolproof way of avoiding it short of marrying someone who does not have it and being faithful to your mate. Think about it. Is sex outside of marriage worth the risks of venereal disease?

Reason 4. The hell on earth of sensual slavery. "Flee fornication. Every sin that a man doeth is without the body; but he that commiteth fornication sinneth against his own body" (1 Cor. 6:18, KJV). The Bible gives us this warning for good reason: Sex is a wonderful servant but a terrible master. As with other pleasures, when regarded solely as an end in itself, sex can get out of control. Instead of us possessing our own bodies and making them do what we want them to do, sex can easily usurp control over us.

What does it mean to say that the immoral person sins against himself? Very simply, when alcoholics or drug addicts get hooked to the point their bodies crave the momentary pleasure that is slowly destroying them, the object of their habit is "outside their own bodies." When that drug enslaves them, their hatred is directed toward the bottle, or a needle, or even a marijuana cigarette. But those who yield their bodies to the control of sexual immorality find that they are hooked on their own bodies. As they discover that their cravings control them, they begin to hate the tyranny of sensuality over their lives, and the object of their hatred easily becomes themselves. An already wounded self-image, scarred from the erosion of self-respect that comes from trivializing sex, is further harmed by the internalization of guilt heaped upon guilt until a person comes to hate himself or herself. Often that person doesn't even know why.

A young man described his addiction to sensuality and the unfulfilled unhappiness he experienced: "When sensuality came to dominate my life, I gave myself over to pornography, masturbation, sexual stimulation with others that led to orgasm without intercourse, and promiscuity. And I discovered that having sex with different partners left me feeling empty. Any relationship that meant something to me soon fell apart.

"The girls who were worth caring about thought too much of themselves to take the risks of sexual exploration for the sake of my gratification. Every girl I really liked was scared by my 'life in the fast lane.'

"When I did have a longer relationship, sex became the all-consuming passion. But the more sex I had with a girl, the less I seemed to respect her or want to be permanently involved with her. I began to wonder if I could ever love or be loved in return."

What this twenty-four-year-old discovered was that undisciplined sensuality and sex are destructive. Only with God's help was he able to turn his life around.

Fire in the fireplace is fine, but in the middle of the living room rug it will burn your house down. That's how sex is. The setting where love can grow and deepen, where sex can be constructive instead of destructive, is a solid, permanent marriage commitment. In the words of Henri Nouwen,

> When the physical encounter of men and women in the intimate act of intercourse is not an expression of their total availability to each other, [what Nouwen calls] the creative fellowship of the weak is not yet reached. Every sexual relationship with built-in reservations, with mental restrictions or time limits, is still part of the taking structure. It means "I want you now, but not tomorrow. I want something from you, but I don't want *you*." Love is limitless. Only when men and women give themselves to each other in total surrender, that is, with their whole person for their whole life, can their encounter bear full fruits.[12]

Why are deeply religious women the most sexually satisfied people in our nation?[13] Because sex is good only with a person with whom you can totally be yourself, without fear of rejection, an unwanted pregnancy, disease, or heartbreak. That is only possible if you know that your partner will be there tomorrow, and every tomorrow thereafter. Only then can you truly give yourself to another, and only through that self-giving commitment can sex fulfill its potential to enrich lives, bringing them closer together instead of further apart.

Sex outside of marriage is a guilt-ridden, alienating experience. Sex within marriage, however, is one of life's richest experiences. I honestly would not trade all the sex I had before marriage for one night of married love with my wife. It would be a poor substitute for the union of body and soul that only the Lord can create between a man and woman who are lovingly committed to one another in marriage.

IS IT WORTH THE RISK?

I understand the temptations that lead people into a self-destructive, immoral life. I also understand the fears that cause people to shrink back from a permanent commitment to another person. People who base their concept of love on romantic notions of falling in or out of love are especially vulnerable to this. Such a view of life encourages a frustrating fickleness that can make people wonder if they ever will be capable of lasting love. The heartbreak so prevalent with today's casual approach to sex and relationships tends to make people feel that a trial sexual relationship can help a couple be sure. "You wouldn't buy shoes unless you tried 'em on," the reasoning goes. The problem is that people aren't a piece of leather. They hurt, they love, they feel intensely, and they deserve to be treated with a great deal of respect and dignity. Ironically, people who live together prior to marriage are just as likely to get divorced as people who do not.

Every person wrestling with the question of premarital sex today needs to ask if it is worth all these risks. Are a few moments of pleasure worth taking a chance on permanent venereal disease, an unwanted pregnancy, the erosion of self-respect, the destruction of love, and the hurt that will be caused to oneself, one's partner, and one's family? Is it worth risking one's education, future, and capacity to love? Is it worth risking the possibility of becoming enslaved to powerful desires and temptations that will control you? These are questions each person must answer for her or himself.

The smartest teens and young adults in America are deciding that Scripture's advice is their best protection against harm.[14]

THE SOLUTION IS OFTEN PART OF THE PROBLEM

One last point needs to be made. Though there is more sex education in our schools than ever before, there are more problems related to sexuality than ever before. While sex education itself is not the problem, amoral sex education contributes to our dilemma. There is clear evidence that where "valueless" sex education is used exclusively, there are more unwanted pregnancies, more abortions and venereal disease, and greater promiscuity.[15]

The material published by Planned Parenthood, a group sponsored largely by huge doles from our taxes, represents the type of literature that is more a part of the problem than a part of the solution. From one chapter comes this hedonistic gem of advice to teenagers:

> Relax about loving. Sex is fun and joyful, and courting is fun and joyful, and it comes in all types and styles, all of which are okay. Do what gives pleasure and ask for what gives pleasure. Don't rob yourself of joy by focusing on old-fashioned ideas about what's normal or nice. Just communicate and enjoy.[16]

Other material they provide asks this poignant rhetorical question: "If you're not supposed to go after a girl for sex, what are you supposed to do?" Their literature discourages children from talking to their parents about sex. It calls people irrational who think homosexuality is wrong, and encourages the acceptance of oral and anal sex as normal parts of adolescent premarital foreplay or a substitute for intercourse. "No one," they say, "has the right to condemn a person on the basis of sexual expression."[17] Does that mean they would say, therefore, we have no right to condemn the perpetrators of rape or incest, or those with a "sexual preference" for sex with animals or children? So much for religious liberty and freedom of expression. Do you want your tax dollars supporting such groups? Do you approve of their philosophy?

167

CONCLUSIONS

A modern writer has said that many contemporary young people approach sex like robots in heat. This mechanistic, compulsive approach to one of the most precious gifts God gave us is a tragic waste. This is the essence of defilement – a lovely and joyful gift profaned by commonality. Had we learned the Bible's lessons from people like Solomon, Amnon, Samson, and others (Ecclesiastes; Proverbs; 2 Sam. 13; Judg. 14-16) sex never would have had to be so tainted, warped, and twisted for so many in the younger generation. Even the prodigal son repented from his wasteful life of debauchery, not because he was afraid of the eternal consequences of his acts, but merely because he came to his senses (Luke 15:11-32). His degenerate circumstances finally revealed to him that unrestrained lust eventually robs a man of all that is worth living for. That is still true today. May our churches and Christian parents garner the courage and find the necessary wisdom to help the next generation avoid the mistakes of the last. If they do, our world can't help but be a better place.

SIXTEEN
CHEATERS NEVER PROSPER, OR HOW ADULT IS ADULTERY?

Many today, women as well as men, are increasingly assailed by the assumption that adultery – unfaithfulness in marriage – is not only OK but even healthy. Many popular magazines have gone so far as to prescribe adultery as an antidote to an unfulfilling marriage. That's akin to recommending amputation for a broken leg. *Cosmopolitan* reports that 54 percent of its readers have had extramarital affairs. Even as conservative a publication as *Ladies' Home Journal* found 21 percent of its readership cheating.[1] As might be expected, the men are even worse. Though I believe its findings are probably distorted, the 1981 *Hite Report on Male Sexuality* claims that nearly 75 percent of today's men have committed adultery.[2]

What is behind the astronomical rise in adultery? Is there anything wrong with it; if so, what? Why is monogamy difficult? How can it be a blessing? These are questions the church has not been prepared to adequately answer. We felt we didn't need to do more than tell people they should be moral "because the Bible says so." Such reasoning is obviously not sufficient for today.

Many unwittingly stumble into the pitfalls of immorality because they are ignorant of the Bible's teachings on the matter. Worldly preachers have so effectively portrayed God as the ultimate permissive parent that many people today don't think he minds their transgressions. People everywhere in modern media are willing to tell the world that things are getting worse because of the legalisms imposed by puritan-minded, religious dinosaurs. A major segment of our society has been willing to forsake historical facts to swallow this line along with the hook and sinker that inevitably accompany it.

What is wrong with adultery? Ironically, most people do not turn to adultery out of any compelling sexual need. Instead they turn to extramarital affairs as a solution to far deeper needs. Adultery has been embraced as a panacea for everything from loneliness and boredom to emotional frigidity and an unrequited desire for intimacy and understanding. More people look to sex beyond their marriage in a quest for compassion rather than passion. It is as likely to be regarded as an ego energizer as it is a sexual release. In adultery's seductive deceptions people search in vain for intimacy apart from involvement, relationship void of responsibility, self-fulfillment without covenant commitment. What they usually end up with is lust without love, and a great deal of heartbreak and loss in the process.

We have already discussed the fact that our greatest needs are much deeper than their physical manifestations. The adulterer usually recognizes this but seeks to fill those needs illegitimately. But a search for instant solutions to one's lack of fulfillment always leaves one worse off than before and compounds the problems.

The Bible warns us that an adulterer never goes unpunished (Prov. 6:29). It also tells us clearly what those punishments will be. And usually, it is never something as obvious as a lightning bolt from heaven. As with fornication, the person committing adultery sins against his own body (1 Cor. 6:18), and eventually painfully experiences the consequences of his transgressions. I have counseled more than my share of adulterers and have yet to meet one whose sin has made them happy or who, when the affair was over, would choose to do it again.

DISASTERS BY THE BAKER'S DOZEN

The awful penalties for adultery go far beyond the obvious threat of venereal disease. The circumstances of life are always polluted as well. A biblical warning against adultery, one that exposes its dangers, is found in Proverbs 6. It was written to keep you from the evil woman, from the smooth tongue of the adulteress. Do not desire her beauty in your heart, nor let her catch you with her eyelids. For on account of a harlot one is reduced to a loaf of bread, and an adulteress hunts for the precious life. Can a man take fire in his bosom, and his clothes not be burned? Or can a man walk on hot coals, and his feet not be scorched? So is the one who goes in to his neighbor's wife; whoever touches her will not go unpunished. The one who commits adultery with a woman is lacking sense; he who would destroy himself does it. Wounds and disgrace he will find, and his reproach will not be blotted out. (vv. 24-29, 32-33)

Many of the dreadful consequences of adultery are catalogued in this passage. In all, I found at least thirteen disasters the Bible forecasts for the adulterer. As Proverbs 6 indicates: (1) a man will be reduced to a loaf of bread. This suggests that he will lose all he has, become nothing more than a meal ticket, and find it difficult to rise above a subsistence level of existence; (2) he will ultimately destroy himself; (3) he will experience wounds (within, to be sure), disgrace, and an irremovable reproach (becoming an object of discredit, shame, and censure).

Other passages predict: (4) the waste of the immoral person's wealth and the consumption of his increase or profits (Prov. 29:3; Job 31:12); (5) a deceptive moral blindness, destroying his ability to understand, hence no capacity for avoiding sin and evil (Hosea 4:2); (6) the inability to return to the paths of (abundant) life (Prov. 21:6); and (7) problems within his own physical body (1 Cor. 6:18).

If the curses stopped there they would be bad enough, but adultery is ultimately a life or death matter (Gen. 20:3). The adulterer (8) will be one of the guests in Sheol (the abode of the dead; not a pleasant place to visit – Prov. 7:27). He will (9) experience great tribulation (Rev. 2:22) in this life and (10) will be cast into the lake of fire reserved for those who transgress moral absolutes (Rev. 21:8). Those who refuse to repent of their adultery (11) cannot (not *will* not) inherit the kingdom of God (1 Cor. 6:9; Gal. 5:2; Eph. 5:5, and elsewhere). Their sin (12) can even infect a whole community of people, leading to their entire destruction (1 Cor. 10:8). That is why adultery is called (13) an "unfruitful deed of darkness" (Eph. 5:3, 11). That may be a classic understatement!

It's no wonder adultery was a capital offense in the Bible (Lev.

20:10) and is dealt with in one of the original Ten Commandments (Exod. 20:14). Few other sins are as attractive, deceitful, or contagious; few carry the potential to overwhelm and destroy individuals and families, and even an entire society.

WHY ADULTERY?

Why do people fall into adultery? The Bible says it is because they are foolish (working against their own best interests) and deceived (blinded to the real and ultimate consequences of their acts – Eph. 5:6). Furthermore, they lack sense and, consequently, fall for their seducer's flattery (Prov. 2:16; 7:5-23). They don't realize that smooth words can lead to a bitter end (Prov. 5:3-4). The adulterous person is cunning, persuasive, and manipulative, a real con artist who searches for a vulnerable, precious life (Prov. 6:26; 7:10). He or she is often religious but lacks the power over temptation that comes from truly knowing God (Prov. 3:13-16). Many Christians are especially vulnerable because in their innocent naiveté, they consider themselves to be safer than they really are (1 Cor. 10:12). This is usually a prelude to disaster, as David and Sampson could willingly testify (2 Sam. 11-17; Ps. 51).

In the last days (which I believe we are in), the Bible warns:

> Men will be lovers of self, lovers of money, boastful, arrogant, revilers, disobedient to parents, ungrateful, unholy, unloving, irreconcilable, malicious gossips, without self-control, brutal, haters of good, treacherous, reckless, conceited, lovers of pleasure rather than lovers of God; holding to a form of godliness, although they have denied its power; and avoid such men as these. For among them are those who enter into households and captivate weak women weighed down with sins, led on by various impulses [controlled by different strong feelings], always learning [enrolled in many continuing education programs] and never able to come to the knowledge of the truth. (2 Tim. 3:2-7)

Such men may be prodded along by their own weak egos, enslaved by insatiable sensual desires, seducing women left and right

172

but never finding fulfillment. What is so deceptive is that these men seldom appear to be the heartless lechers they are. They have probably learned to be kind and polite. They even appear to be religious and sensitive. In reality, though, it's all a ploy. They understand too well most women's weaknesses. These women are likely to become vulnerable to the emotional longings and desires these men are prone to stir. However, they are no less enslaved and consumed than they would be if their bondage were sexually oriented. In fact, emotional lust can get a stronger grip on a person than sexual.

I know of a young pastor who, while traveling, almost fell into an adulterous relationship with a Christian woman. Though he never even kissed her, an emotional bond developed between them that he said made all physical lust seem feeble in comparison. Fortunately for both of them, they came to their senses, and after sharing the problem openly with their mates, developed a strategy for changing the circumstances that might have led to a devastating relationship. Without God's help and their willingness to bring the problem to light, two marriages and a promising pastoral career were almost shattered.

Unless a person repents of these strong feelings and controlling lusts, he or she will never regain control of his or her life. The deceitfulness of sins that promise only temporary satisfaction has lured many an unsuspecting victim into a lifetime of heartbreak and privation. Certainly the wages of such sins can never be enough to compensate for the suffering they unavoidably produce.

Another man I know had problems because his sexual drive was much greater than his wife's. He entered into a relationship with a young woman on a purely physical basis, only later to find himself deeply in love with her.

It's easy to love the other woman – she's always available. In the blindness of new "love" her blemishes are sure to be obscured. Ann Landers recently ran a letter from a man who said he made the awful mistake of divorcing his first wife to marry the other woman. He said it was the worst mistake of his life, and he knew many men who would say the same thing.

Though the man I knew didn't marry the other woman, his relationship with her almost destroyed his relationship with God, totally destroyed his peace of mind for a couple of years, and came very close to causing him to lose the love and respect of his wife and children. It certainly didn't help him with his need for either sex or love.

Adultery is an attempt to gain satisfaction beyond the marriage, that, in fact, can be derived only from the marriage. The adulterer may be seeking fulfillment for his ego, emotional needs, or sexual drives, but the fact remains that when a person looks beyond his mate, he is looking for love in the wrong place.

REAL LOVE: SACRIFICIAL LOVE

Real love is found by people who learn to love sacrificially. If a person can deny selfish need and consider if his or her actions are related to the mate's inability or unwillingness to meet that need, then that person can find the Lord's way to true and lasting satisfaction. Not only will that person avoid the catalogue of problems that eventually overtake the adulterer, but he or she will also escape the spillover of those problems onto others. The marriage can be salvaged and the mate, children, and family of his or her potential illicit partner spared much heartbreak.

God so loved that he gave – even to the point of ultimate self-denial and sacrifice. The man and woman who can similarly learn redemptive love in the midst of their disappointment, pain, emptiness, and frustration will be well on the way to finding real love. In the process they will discover the kind of satisfaction that is known only by those who live as God intended them to live – as children of the heavenly King. For them no sacrifice is too great, for the kingdom of heaven is theirs. They are its princes and princesses. By virtue of Christ's righteousness they have become its rightful heirs (Rom. 8:10-17).

We must rembember that the dominance of monogamy paralled the rise of New Testament Christianity. Only people who personally know the love and faithfulness of a covenant God can faithfully maintain a permanent covenant relationship with their mate. That is the reason why so many secular psychologists prescribe divorce as the solution to marital problems. The same reasoning in our humanistic medical community prescribes death as a solution to those having birth defects. Without the power of the Holy Spirit in a person's life the self-denial required for redemptive problem-solving is too difficult. Without Christ's Spirit fulfilling and strengthening the inner man, it is impossible to overcome the lusts and desires daily assailing the outer man in our modern world.

We must realize the futility of seeking to solve all of our world's problems through legislation. Morality can be legislated. All legislation is the prescription of one moral position or another. The myth that "you can't legislate morality" is an absurd contradiction in terms akin to the hypocritical belief that "there are no absolutes."

What is true, however, is that you cannot enforce morality. It is essentially a matter of the heart (Mark 7:20-23).

THE ANSWER? SALVATION

If we want to see our world change, moral coercion is not the ultimate answer. Nothing short of a profound spiritual revolution in the hearts of people can avert the ultimate, total collapse of our culture. Sin has always been a greater enemy than Mongol hordes or economic turbulence could ever be to civilization. The only solution to sin is salvation.

I am not speaking here only of conversion. Conversion is just the beginning of salvation. Jesus came to "save His people from their sins" (Matt. 1:21) by teaching us how to be "righteous, just as He is righteous" (1 John 3:7). Nothing less than a holistic salvation, one that permeates the lives, values, and priorities of all God's people, is sufficient.

Such a thorough-going salvation must begin in the people of God. Judgment must begin first among God's own children (1 Pet. 4:17). The Church must also be the spawning ground for redemption. If the Church were to become fully Christ-centered, society could still be saved. Religion alone cannot save us. In fact, it is part of our problem. Our world is waiting to *see* righteousness. It is looking for conversion that changes communities, decisions that lead to discipleship, love that is reflected in life-style. Until these things are evident in the people of God, the Church will continue to be irrelevant for most of our society. Until we learn to genuinely love one another with the love of Christ we deserve to be ignored.

What does all this have to do with immorality? The people of God have been a spiritually adulterous congregation. The sensual seduction of society at large is in direct proportion to the idolatry and apostasy of the Church. Its repentance is likewise conditional upon its restoration. Only a righteous remnant can bring redemption to a deceived pagan culture.

God is intent upon having a holy bride for his heavenly Groom. We have much faithlessness from which we need to repent. Until the Church takes Christ and his Word more seriously, we have little to say to our world that we do not need to hear ourselves. Recent studies have shown that there is almost as much adultery, premarital sex, and divorce in the Church as there is in the world.

The Lord is interested in far more than insulating us against lust. He wants his people to realize that the sins the people in our world commit are directly related to the love his people have been lacking. He is calling us to be spiritually faithful; to be an example of the holy, sacrificial love Christ showed to this sin-sick world.

If we will be true to him, the world will find it increasingly difficult to live with its falsehood. There will be a light to lead the way out of darkness, a love that can make lust seem pale and tarnished in comparison, a people in whom God will be pleased to dwell. Then and only then can faithfulness become an antidote to adultery.

SEVENTEEN
ABORTION: THE
HIDDEN HOLOCAUST

Twenty years ago the Church overwhelmingly agreed that abortion was wrong. Today we are not so sure. Some liberal denominations actively lobby for unrestricted abortion rights. Most congregations have women in their midst who have had an abortion, and, as a result, many people in the church are frustrated or confused about where to stand or what to do about this issue. Clearly, more scriptural teaching about this frightening social phenomenon is needed.

Some say the Bible is silent about abortion. This is technically true. The word is never mentioned in its pages. That's because the Hebrews knew what God's law taught about life, its origins, and the shedding of innocent blood and would never have thought of adopting the pagan abortion practices of their neighbors.

It is time we examined abortion through the microscope of the Scriptures. If Christians took a biblical stand on this issue, the Supreme Court's infamous decision of 1973 *(Roe v. Wade)* would be reversed, and the more than 1.5 million lives per year being destroyed by this holocaust would be saved. Perhaps the deserved judgment of God on our terrible blood-guiltiness might be averted as well.

WHEN LIFE BEGINS

It is commonly agreed that a woman has a right to her own body; the state should not tell her what to do with it. I have no quarrel with that. Christians don't have an unquestionable mandate to dictate the sexual morality of their nonbelieving neighbors. The foundation for all social law, however, is this: my right to swing my fist stops with the end of your nose. The law must protect you from being harmed by the irresponsible or inconsiderate exercise of my personal liberty. In abortion, we are dealing with another human life, and it deserves to be protected.

Does the Bible say anything definitive about when human life begins? Yes! Listen to the clear and powerful testimony of Psalm 139:13, 15-16:

> For Thou didst form my inward parts; Thou didst weave me in my mother's womb. . . . My frame was not hidden from Thee, when I was made in secret, and skillfully wrought in the depths of the earth. Thine eyes have seen my unformed substance; and in Thy book they were all written, the days that were ordained for me, when as yet there was not one of them.

Other Scriptures point to the reality of preborn life. Jeremiah 1:4-5 is another prime example:

> Now the word of the Lord came to me saying, "Before I formed you in the womb I knew you, and before you were born I consecrated you; I have appointed you a prophet to the nations."

How many, I fear to wonder, are the prophets, statesmen, and good solid working people whose lives have been extinguished by abortion before they were born?

Like Pharaoh's slaughter of the innocents prior to Moses' birth, and Herod's vain attempt to eradicate Jesus, our generation has witnessed an unprecedented outpouring of wrath against the helpless innocents. Their blood cries out to a righteous God for vindication. How long can his judgment be forestalled?

At the union of the egg and sperm, all that is necessary for the embryo to become a mature adult is present. The only thing needed for development is nutrition. Each fertilized egg is a unique and distinct individual with a genetic makeup completely separate from its parents. He or she may even have a different blood type. At ten weeks this little one has ten fingers and toes, a heartbeat, brain waves, and the capacity to taste sweet and sour and distinguish pain. If the egg of a bald eagle deserves the law's protection, why doesn't this child (Lev. 24:21)? The unborn child is a separate human life apart from a woman's body.

Every generation of Christians except the present one has agreed that the crime of abortion is a heinous one, but many think they know better today. Will we never learn from history? Surely Proverbs 24:11, 12 must be addressed to us when it says we must

> deliver those who are being taken away to death, and those who are staggering to slaughter, O hold them back. If you say, "See, we did not know this," does He not consider it who weighs the hearts? And does He not know it who keeps your soul? And will He not render to man according to his work?

God knows if Christians bury their heads in the sand on this issue, he will have to apologize to Hilter for his judgment on Germany—and their killing was not done for money. Those who perform abortions for profit would do well to heed the warnings of Proverbs 1:18-19. Those who shed innocent blood for money "lie in wait for their own blood; they ambush their own lives. So are the ways of everyone who gains by violence; it takes away the life of its possessors."

DOES THE BIBLE ADDRESS THE ABORTION ISSUE?

The Bible is lucid in its condemnation of those who shed innocent blood (Deut. 19:10-13). "Hands that shed innocent blood" is one of the six things the Lord hates (Prov. 6:17). Especially repugnant to God was the offering of human sacrifices (Lev. 20:2-5). The Canaanite practice of offering up their children to be burned in the fires to their impotent deities was one of the main reasons why the Lord dispossessed them from the Promised Land (Deut. 12:28-32).

Can we in America expect to retain his blessing upon us if we similarly adopt the ways of the heathen? What difference is there between the ancient pagans who threw their children into the fiery volcano and those in our society who burn the skin off their own unborn through saline abortions? Are our idols of education, comfort, prosperity, and expedience more worthy than Molech or Baal?

How far we have come from being a nation where children are considered "a [blessed] gift of the Lord" (Ps. 127:3-5). Even as a Christian I, too, was confused about abortion. My wife and I were going to wait five years to have children, and then four came in the first six years despite our careful use of birth control measures. After the first two we secretly considered abortion, but thank God we didn't go through with it. No one had helped us realize what a blessed treasure children are. Our antichild society had blinded us to the unparalleled joys they can bestow upon a family.

How ridiculous that environmentalists are concerned for the preservation of snail darters (small, near-extinct fish) but not for people. It's a strange contradiction, indicative of the kind of confusion in which our age is immersed. We have forgotten that human life, made in the image of our Creator (Gen. 1:27), is of infinitely greater worth than that of other creatures (Lev. 24:21).

Someday we may find that the pseudoscience of Darwinism has robbed us of much more than we thought. By throwing the Genesis narratives into disrepute, we have eroded the core values that enable us to become a truly civilized and valuable society. When the unborn are no longer sacred, the retarded, disabled, and aged can also become endangered. After they are violated, if history continues, it is anyone's guess as to who will be the next class of people our culture will decide unworthy of life.

WHAT ABOUT WOMEN?

When I was on a television talk show, the woman interviewing me was astonished to learn that I would be pro-life even if I didn't care about the sanctity of life or the destruction of the unborn. I would oppose abortion, if for no other reason, on the basis of what it does to women. Abortion is a classic example of how a woman's desire for comfort ultimately works against her own best interests.

When I argued in favor of abortion, I did so believing the pro-abortion propaganda mythology that said thousands of women die each year at the hands of illegal abortionists. Dr. Bernard Nathanson, a pro-life advocate who once ran the nation's largest abortion clinic, says those figures were totally contrived. He and others who had sought to legitimize abortions fed such fallacies to an unquestioning media in the late sixties, deliberately lying to establish their case for abortion. In an average year before abortion was legalized, about 160 women died at the hands of back-alley butchers.[1] It's possible that as many are still dying today from complications arising from legal abortions, but the confidentiality of abortion records makes these figures impossible to substantiate. The actual number may be much higher.

About 100 other medical complications may arise from abortion, including as much as a 10 percent chance of infertility.[2] Psychological factors include a 400 percent increase in the suicide rate of women who have had abortions.[3] But the most amazing harm abortion does to women relates to their inner well-being.

A rather enigmatic Scripture that sheds some light on this area for us is 1 Timothy 2:15. Until I understood the biblical definition of salvation, this passage was a complete mystery to me. It says, "Women shall be preserved [literally 'saved'] through the bearing of children if they continue in faith and love and sanctity with self-restraint." At first glance it appears that this passage teaches that a woman's eternal destiny depends on her bearing children. But to think this way is to miss the point. Salvation, biblically defined, is as concerned with temporal realities as it is with those eternal. It literally means delivered from sin, set free to live righteously, and empowered to attain to completion and wholeness in God.[4]

As I considered this definition of salvation in light of the passage in 1 Timothy, I saw something very important to the total well-being of a godly woman. Bearing children does for a woman what being a godly husband does for a man. It sets her free from slavery to counterproductive selfish instincts that wage war against her real well-being.

Here's what I mean. As we have already discussed, our deepest need is love. The greatest barrier to its fulfillment, our selfishness, prevents us from living consistently with our true nature as people made in the image of the self-giving God who is love. When a man consents to love his wife as Christ loved the Church and gave himself up for her (Eph. 5:25), his selfishness is mortally wounded. The same thing happens when a woman bears children. It is impossible for a woman to bear and raise children well and not deal with her inner selfishness. If she is to succeed at being a mother, her selfishness must die.

181

In this strange paradoxical way that's at the core of kingdom living, childbearing reverses the curse that was put upon women by the Fall. This is again similar to what happens in men. The curses that were put upon them include expulsion from the Garden of Eden, the responsibility for leading their family, and earning their bread by the sweat of their brow. Men who seek to regain paradise by abdicating their responsibilities and avoiding work only create for themselves a meaningless, living hell.

Similarly, as a result of the Fall, women have been cursed with a desire for their husbands (who will rule over them) and pain in childbearing (Gen. 3:16). Women in support of the feminist movement who resist their husband's headship swim upstream against reality, ignoring biblical mandates to do otherwise (1 Cor. 11:3; Eph. 5:22-24). Their husbands will either rule over them with a heavy hand or through neglect abdicate their God-given responsibility to love their wives as Christ loved the Church (Eph. 5:25-31).

Women who would seek to avoid the curse and pain of bearing and raising children, either by refusing to have children or by handing them over to someone else to raise, are rejecting the salvation that can be theirs only through motherhood. This particular aspect of God's salvation is uniquely designed to save her from her own counterproductive, selfish instincts. It is as essential to her to mortify her selfishness as it is for a man to lay down his life for his wife.

Unless selfishness is dealt a fatal blow, no amount of personal freedom or carnal self-indulgence can satisfy us. Parties, luxuries, trips to the Caribbean, even cocaine and illicit sex are all inadequate. Those who despise the cross – not the one on which Christ died, but the one he invites us to carry as we follow him (Matt. 16:24) – will remain in bondage to an increasing, vain need for an ever-elusive inner satisfaction. Instead of the power of the Resurrection that alone can make them righteous, they will find themselves broken, empty, and miserable in the midst of all they thought would bring them happiness and fulfillment.

Many modern women are beginning to discover something of the real source of genuine fulfillment for themselves. In a fascinating TV interview, jet-setter Gloria Vanderbilt was asked what she considered her greatest accomplishment. This woman who had lived in splendor all over the world, who had had successful careers that enabled her to achieve wealth and fame, so stunned the interviewer with her answer that the producer immediately cut to another segment. Her greatest achievement? "Being a mother!"

Many unfortunates in our age are learning the truth of the Scripture that says one of the most insatiable things in all of life is a barren womb (Prov. 30:16). The abortion mentality has robbed women of children or, worse, the ability to appreciate them. How many will go to their graves broken, miserable, lonely, and painfully empty? And what they had sought was wholeness and fulfillment.

THE CHURCH'S COMPLICITY

The Church has complied, both consciously and unwittingly, with the hidden holocaust. The young woman who successfully argued before the Supreme Court in favor of abortion-on-demand in the case of *Roe v. Wade* is the daughter of a pastor. She said she did so as a "righteous" extension of the concern for "justice" that she had learned from her father's ministry.

A key Supreme Court justice who was instrumental in penning the notorious 1973 *Roe v. Wade* decision is a United Methodist. He said he did so with the support of the Protestant community. In fact, in 1972, the United Methodist Church reversed its long-standing Christian tradition against abortion. In language couched with sympathy and regret, it accepted abortion-on-demand and even inferred that in some instances it is a righteous decision. One United Methodist bureaucrat called her abortion the holiest experience of her life.

Other denominations agreed. The Religious Concern for Abortion Rights lists among its supporters the American Baptist Church, Disciples of Christ, Episcopal Women's Caucus, Lutheran Church in America, Presbyterian Church in the United States, United Church of Christ, United Methodist Church, United Presbyterian U.S.A., and the YMCA. In a recent year the United Methodist Church alone gave more than $400,000 to support pro-choice causes.

Probably more significant than what has been mentioned is the unwitting way that the Christian community has created an atmosphere in which abortion becomes desirable.

Mainly we have failed dismally in our attempts to educate our own people about sexuality. It seems sex can be discussed today anywhere but in church. The suffering our bashfulness on the topic has caused is monumental. God is not afraid to talk about sex. His Word is full of wise, sound, balanced counsel. We need to teach it to our people and help them experience the benefits of our heavenly Father's eternal wisdom. Books like this should be established texts in churches and in Christian schools and colleges. Parents should be trained to teach their children what God's Word says. If God's people do not understand his perspective on sex, they will be unable to share God's truth with those who need salvation.

Even more important, however, the atmosphere, focus, and ministry of the Church must change dramatically. It is tragic that the last place many people would go to receive help with an unwanted pregnancy is their church. Most parents would be devastated if their home congregation discovered their unwed daughter's pregnancy. This should not be the case. The Church of Jesus Christ should be a hospital for sinners. People should feel free to turn to the body of Christ for mercy, compassion, grace, and practical help. The proliferation of pregnancy centers, Alcoholics Anonymous groups, Overeaters Anonymous, and other such organizations is evidence of the Church's failure to deal with these problems. A true church, one patterned after the life and ministry of Jesus of Nazareth, will be a "sinner's anonymous." People with all varieties of diseases, afflictions, and bondages should be able to look to the Church for mercy, compassion, and the kind of genuine deliverance that sets captives free. Indeed there is victory available in Jesus.

My congregation includes victims of incest, abortion, promiscuity, and sexual abuse. Former drug abusers, schizophrenics, alcoholics, and unwed mothers have found the deliverance, inner healing, acceptance, and true liberation that are all different dimensions of a full-orbed gospel of salvation. We apply biblical principles to our families, finances, and all other significant areas of our lives. Vineyard and Covenant Fellowships all over the world do the same. People who have been virtually unreachable through medicine, psychology, and traditional religion are joyfully embracing the call of Christ's kingdom and becoming whole.

God's people must be willing to not only change their attitudes but their life-styles and priorities. We must forsake empty religious rituals and replace them with the authentic sacrificial righteousness the Lord requires of his people. Isaiah speaks of God's chosen fast. Authentic, efficacious self-denial is "to loosen the bonds of wickedness, to undo the bands of the yoke, and to let the oppressed go free, and break every yoke" (Isa. 58:6).

Railing against the apostasies of liberation theology will be in vain unless the Church begins to heal broken sinners. An "acceptable day of the Lord" is one in which God's people "divide [their] bread with the hungry, and bring the homeless poor into [their] house; when [they] see the naked, cover him; and [do] not hide [themselves] from [their] own flesh . . ." (Isa. 58:7). Many marvelous promises are bequeathed to those who will "remove the yoke from [their] midst, the pointing of the finger, and speaking wickedness, and if [they] give [themselves – not the local church food pantry] to the hungry, and satisfy the desire of the afflicted . . ." (vv. 9-10). Some would wonder if these mandates are normative in the New Testament. I can only refer them to the Sermon on the Mount, Matthew 25, and the Books of James and 1 John.

If churches would educate their people, demand an end to their denomination's support of abortion-on-demand, vote for pro-life candidates, and become a haven for the brokenhearted, the hidden holocaust could be stopped. Most important, the Church must become a place where people can find mercy instead of condemnation, sins forgiven instead of condoned, and concrete care instead of irrelevant religious rituals. If that happens, the Church will change the world.

Abortion is the ultimate rebellion against the authority of God, the next-to-the-last assertion of man's autonomy. By it he denies his responsibility to the most innocent and helpless among us.

Those who defend abortion assent to the heresy of the sexual revolution, which is basically the belief that man will find happiness through the unrestrained indulgence of his sexuality. By twisted bits of mistaken assumptions, some feminists insist that abortion is the only way they can be free to enjoy sex as irresponsibly as men. Ironically, they have somehow failed to notice how little men are enjoying their so-called freedom.

Any person who claims to be a Christian and fails to see the demonic nature behind the abortion mentality is so self-deceived that only a thoroughgoing repentance can save his or her soul. Abortion is indeed a "sin unto death" of the worst kind. Those who know it is happening and do nothing to stop it are probably worse off than those who don't yet understand why it's so wrong.

Everyone who knows abortion is wrong should be doing something to stop it. It's no longer enough to be tacitly pro-life. Everyone can do something, and the totality of our efforts could put an end to this horrendous act against humanity. I pray we won't be greeted on the far side of eternity by millions of unborn children saying, "I couldn't cry, but you knew, and you did nothing to stop it."

EIGHTEEN
GAY AGONY:
THE TRUTH ABOUT
HOMOSEXUALITY

The latest moral boundaries that our secular humanist social architects desire to erase are our mores against homosexuality. Since organized religion "is probably the single most influential factor in the evaluation of behavior"[1] and remains "the validator of the behavior of choice,"[2] homosexuals work fervently to legitimize their cause in the eyes of religious people. Experts agree that "the main stumbling block in the theoretical and practical acceptance [of homosexuality] by American society has been traditional religion."[3] Because of the intense lobbying efforts directed toward churches, many Christians are perplexed about homosexuality.

Some mainline church bureaucrats have attempted to make the homosexual movement a civil rights issue. Those who oppose homosexuality's legitimacy are called judgmental and unloving. Deliberately deceptive language, the ambivalence of biblically corrupt liberal churches in search of a new cause, and the reluctance of many conservative Christians to discuss sexuality have all contributed to the confusion.

It is time for a frank, biblical examination of homosexuality. We need to understand the causes of homosexuality and the consequences of accepting it. Only then can we appreciate the cure that is available through Christ.

WHAT CAUSES HOMOSEXUALITY?
Though homosexuals would have you believe otherwise, there is absolutely no scientific evidence that some people are born with a

homosexual orientation.[4] Many psychiatrists are concluding that homosexuals are made, not born. Typical of the honest conclusions of the scientific community is the statement that "genetic, hereditary, constitutional, glandular, or hormonal factors have no significance in causing homosexuality."[5] Even when a different body chemistry is found in homosexuals, there is no way of establishing whether it is the cause or effect of their homosexuality.

Dr. Irwin Bieber, a psychiatrist recognized as one of America's leading authorities on homosexuality, says that homosexuals "are made that way largely by their parents."[6] A psychologist once said he had never met a homosexual who had a good relationship with his father, or a person who had a good relationship with his father who became a homosexual.

Homosexual tendencies almost certainly are a consequence of defective parenting. A passive, detached, or absent father inclines children toward a homosexual life-style. Inappropriate mothering is also problematic. Domineering or "smother mothers" tend to push their children toward a homosexual orientation. Of 106 male homosexuals interviewed, 81 had domineering mothers, 62 were overprotected, 66 had been their parents' favorite child, 82 had fathers who spent little time with their sons, and 79 had fathers who were emotionally detached from their children.[7]

David F. Busby lists nine defective family patterns that can cause homosexual and lesbian tendencies: (1) absence of intimacy between mother and father; (2) a father who is absent, through death or divorce, coupled with a mother who is too present; (3) a punitive father and a masochistic mother; (4) a passive father and a domineering mother who is either overprotective or too permissive; (5) an aloof father and a mother who is too close and overinvolved; (6) a vulgar father and a prudish mother to whom sex appears reprehensible; (7) both parents absent before age twelve; (8) an idealized mother and a blockage in the child's ability to identify with the father; (9) an idealized father (or older brother) resulting in a hostile-dependency relationship with the father.[8]

There are different configurations of a situation where "mother's influence demasculinized the son and stripped the father of masculine qualities and/or the father made identification with himself unpalatable."[9] A lesbian tells of a harsh, stern father who was cruel to her mother. She grew up despising men except for her older brother whom she idolized and sought to imitate in every respect.[10] A homosexual tells of a father who was impossible to please. He needed men's acceptance and turned, eventually, to homosexual affairs as a means of securing it.[11] Another lesbian talks of a boyfriend who tried to rape her. She vowed never to let any man have control of her life.[12]

Other factors contribute to a homosexual or lesbian orientation. Success ruined Sodom. Ezekiel 16:49 tells us that Sodom's root sins were pride, abundance of bread, and too much misspent idle time. Instead of helping the poor and needy, the people chose to live selfishly, concerned only with their own needs and desires. This led to boredom with normal sensuality and opened them up to the perverse lusts that precipitated their demise.

Tim LaHaye says that a melancholy temperament, permissive childhood training, insecurity about one's sexual identity, childhood sexual experiences, an early preoccupation with sex, youthful masturbation and sexual fantasizing, and peer group pressure can add up to leading a child astray.[13]

We dare not forget to mention here also that homosexuals do seek to lure young recruits into their life-style. Studies show that "in societies where homosexuality is lauded or approved it will be more prevalent."[14] Sociologist J. T. Landis at the University of Berkeley interviewed 1,800 students. Five hundred had been approached by homosexuals. Two-thirds of these attempts occurred before the students were sixteen.[15] In another study 979 homosexuals were interviewed. Twenty-five percent admitted to having sex with boys age fifteen or younger. A campus minister at a large state university told me that the biggest barrier to his evangelistic efforts came not from cults, but from a mainline denomination's campus ministry where homosexuals were allowed to openly recruit for their life-style.

Our society is engaged in a fierce struggle to redefine its moral boundary lines. Committed Christians must enter the political and public arenas where these struggles take place locally and nationally. We must fight to retain biblical standards of absolutes. If we don't, there is no telling if or when our downward moral slide will be stopped. There is already an organization, comprised mostly of homosexuals, called the Pedophile Information Exchange (PIE). Their agenda? Fighting for the legitimizing of their "sexual orientation." Their preference? Sex with children. Their goal? Lowering of the age of consent.[16]

The effects of moral shifts in public opinion are never immediately obvious. Christians have failed to fight for biblical values related to divorce, premarital sex, and abortion in the recent past. Today few families are untouched by the devastating fallout from these decisions. Consequences that are at least as damaging will be sure to follow if we withdraw on homosexual issues as well.

As noted previously, the argument that you can't legislate morality is as absurd as the statement that there are no absolutes. Morality is defined as "principles of right and wrong in conduct." In that sense all laws legislate morality. It is true that you can't force people to abide by laws governing private sexual conduct. The law, however, is a powerful teacher. It can go a long way toward establishing society's mores. That is why homosexuals fight so hard to change the law and why we need to work to see that they don't succeed.

The Lord tells us homosexuality is really the symptom of a more significant disorientation: idolatry. In Romans 1:18-32, we are told that the truth about God—his existence and eternal power—is known to men instinctively, for God made it evident to all. Those who by their sinful acts suppress the truth are therefore without excuse. For though they knew God, they did not honor him. Consequently, they became futile in their speculations, and their hearts (the seat of desire) became dark and confused. Professing wisdom, they unwittingly became fools. They rejected living as people made in God's image. Instead of embracing selfless love and holiness as their true identity, they emulated the sensuality of beasts, identifying themselves with their lower carnal nature.

The Lord's response? He left their awful freedom intact. He allowed them to pursue their lusts and to become morally, spiritually, and physically defiled by their degrading passions. Worshiping the creature instead of the Creator, they eventually exchanged their natural desires for abnormal ones.

THE CONSEQUENCES

As with all transgressions of the moral law there are predictable, inevitable consequences of homosexuality. The wrath of God, which is initially revealed in the consequences of disobedience, carries with it many penalties in this life. Romans 1 commences with a catalogue of those problems, not the least of which is "being filled with all unrighteousness, wickedness, greed, evil; full of envy, murder, strife, deceit, malice; they are gossips, slanderers, haters of God, insolent, arrogant, boastful, inventors of evil, disobedient to parents, without understanding, untrustworthy, unloving, unmerciful" (vv. 29-31). Ask a homosexual if those sins reflect the homosexual life-style. Those I have talked with often describe their experiences with the homosexual community in precisely these terms.

It's no wonder a reporter once said, "Whoever decided to call homosexuals 'gay' must have had a terrible sense of humor."[17] Historian Arthur M. Schlesinger went even further: "Gay used to be one of the most agreeable words in the language. Its appropriation by a notably morose group is an act of piracy."[18] Indeed the author of Proverbs couldn't be more on target when he says, "He who is perverted in his language falls into evil" (Prov. 17:20). A cursory exploration into the murky underworld of the homosexual subculture should make one thing painfully obvious: No informed person could in good conscience call homosexuals gay.

What is their life-style like? As mentioned previously, even the secular magazine *Psychology Today* estimates that the average male homosexual has sex with at least five hundred partners in his lifetime. The average lesbian, reflecting a woman's tendency to value emotional gratification above the physical, still has five partners in her lifetime.[19] In addition, it is estimated that 20 to 50 percent of the homosexual community has some kind of venereal disease, in some cases fatal.[20] At this writing more than twenty-five hundred have died from AIDS, and that number is expected to skyrocket. Many compare the astronomical growth in AIDS-related deaths to the scourge of the black plague which decimated over half the population of some areas of the world in the fourteenth century.

Other problems, less directly of a sexual nature, also plague the homosexual. Their own literature often discusses a gnawing loneliness that often must be anesthetized with drugs and alcohol. One psychologist probably exaggerates only slightly when he says, "Not every alcoholic is a homosexual, but every homosexual is an alcoholic."[21]

The Bible is frighteningly accurate in calling homosexuality a "hateful abomination" (Lev. 18:22). Most homosexuals are filled with hatred for themselves and others. The noisy desperation described by psychiatrist Melvin Anchell leaves little room for much else. He says that "homosexuals are seldom satisfied with their relationships and are constantly seeking new thrills, or new forms of sexuality. They head into sadomasochism. They are frequently vicious with their own partners and with others."[22] A testimony to this is the violent hatred homosexuals express toward people such as Anita Bryant and others who criticize their insatiable lusts. Connaught Marshner says that of 518 deaths in mass murders involving sex over the past seventeen years in the United States, homosexuals killed at least 68 percent of the victims. Forty-four percent of the murderers were bisexual or homosexual.

Dr. Daniel Cappon, a psychiatrist who has treated hundreds of homosexuals, says:

> Homosexuality, by definition, is not healthy or wholesome. . . . The homosexual person, at best, will be unhappier and more unfulfilled than the sexually normal person. There are emotional and physical consequences to this protracted state of mental dissatisfaction. At worst, the homosexual person will die younger and suffer emotional, mental and physical illness more often than the normal person. The natural history of the homosexual person seems to be one of frigidity, impotence, broken personal relationships, psychosomatic disorders, alcoholism, paranoia psychosis, and suicide. . . . [23]

Homosexuals argue that their sufferings are an outgrowth of the social ostracism they experience because of an outdated biblical view. Ignoring the scientific evidence, they try to convince themselves that the Lord made them the way they are. They maintain that the Bible does not really condemn homosexuality, just promiscuity and cult prostitution. Let us examine the biblical data to see if those assertions are correct. Scripture's teachings and pronouncements offer clarity as a refreshing contrast to the contrived complexities of the secular worldview.

THE BIBLICAL DATA

Pro-homosexual exegetes argue that there may have been an affair between David and Jonathan (1 Sam. 18:1-4; 2 Sam. 1:25-27). Some even go so far as to suggest that Jesus and the Apostle John, "the beloved disciple," were homosexual lovers. But as Enrique T. Rueda maintains, "The reading of a sexual affair between them is absolutely gratuitous and unwarranted; it assumes that all strong personal relationships are sexual in nature. . . . In no instance does the Bible speak favorably of homosexuality."[24]

While many biblical passages condemn the practice of using male and female cult prostitutes in the temple (Deut. 23:17; 1 Kings 14:24; 15:12; and 22:46 for example), this is by no means the only form of homosexuality the Bible condemns. Genesis 19 portrays God's judgment on Sodom and Gomorrah, from which comes our use of the word *sodomy* as a description of abnormal sexual intercourse. Homosexuals claim that the sin for which Sodom was judged was inhospitality. The Bible indicates that the problem was more severe than that. When angels visited Lot, "The men of Sodom, surrounded the house, both young and old, all the people from every quarter [literally, "without exception"]; and they called to Lot and said to him, 'Where are the men who came to you tonight? Bring them out to us that we may have relations [literally, "have intercourse"] with them' " (vv. 4-5). Those same men later attempted to break into Lot's house to rape them, at which point the angels intervened. Judges 19:22-25 relates a remarkably similar encounter later in Israel's history as men forgot the lessons of Sodom.

Other passages specifically catalogue the Lord's prohibitions against homosexuality. Leviticus 18:22 says, "You shall not lie with a male as one lies with a female; it is an abomination." The penalty prescribed for those who do? "If there is a man who lies with a male as those who lie with a woman, both of them have committed a detestable act; they shall surely be put to death. Their bloodguiltiness is upon them" (Lev. 20:13).

While Christians in a pluralistic culture cannot expect the death penalty for immoral acts, it is obvious that the Lord regarded such sins as a serious threat to his people and purposes.

Homosexuality and other forms of sexual immorality are tenacious and contagious sins. Those who engaged in such acts in the midst of God's people were to be cut off from them in an exemplary public fashion. In this way, as God mediated his judgment through his delegated earthly authorities, his people would be preserved from perversion. The fear of the Lord acted as their protection.

Are these Old Testament prohibitions still relevant? Homosexuals point out that Jesus never spoke against homosexuality. They apparently have forgotten that he said,

> Do not think that I came to abolish the Law or the Prophets; I did not come to abolish, but to fulfill. For truly I say to you, *until heaven and earth pass away*, not the smallest letter or stroke shall pass from the Law, until all is accomplished. Whoever then annuls one of the least of these commandments, and so teaches others, shall be called least in the kingdom of heaven; but whoever keeps and teaches them, he shall be called great in the kingdom of heaven. For I say to you, that unless your righteousness surpasses that of the scribes and Pharisees, you shall not enter the kingdom of heaven. (Matt. 5:17-20)

Imagine what he would say of those who violated greater commandments, those the Bible calls "sins unto death" (1 John 5:16-17, KJV).

The apostles Paul and John clearly taught that homosexuality and other immoral acts are in this category. In Galatians 5:19 Paul says that "sexual immorality, impurity and sensuality," among other absolute sins, are transgressions that will keep a person from inheriting God's kingdom (v. 21). He tells us in 1 Timothy 1 that the law is made for fornicators and homosexuals (v. 9). The law is a tutor (Gal. 3:24) to bring them to Christ. From him they can find the power to overcome their sins (1 John 3:3-10) and live a righteous life.

Paul asks the Corinthians if they don't know that "the unrighteous shall not inherit the kingdom of God." He warns them against deception in these matters: "Neither fornicators, nor idolators, nor adulterers, nor effeminate [by perversion], nor homosexuals, nor thieves, nor the covetous, nor drunkards, nor revilers, nor swindlers, shall inherit the kingdom of God." He then holds out these marvelous words of promise: "And such were some of you; but you were washed, but you were sanctified, but you were justified in the name of the Lord Jesus Christ, and in the Spirit of our God" (1 Cor. 6:9-11).

THE CURE

Many read bad news into the Bible's unwavering proclamation that homosexuality is a sin. Actually the opposite is true. If homosexuality were a God-given orientation, people could not change. They would be forever locked into this torturously frustrating and degrading life-style. If it is a sin, however, there is hope. Jesus came to save people from their sins (Matt. 1:21). I have personally ministered to homosexuals who later testified that with God's help their alleged homosexual orientation was changed. He had made them truly free (John 8:31-36). Nothing is impossible for him (Matt. 19:26; Phil. 4:13).

Speaking of the very passage from Corinthians that we have considered, a young homosexual wrote, "When I came to this significant statement in 1 Corinthians 6:11, I underlined. I read and reread. Then I broke down and cried and said, 'Thank God,' because this gave me hope. Those few words brought me new confidence."[25]

Many homosexuals will do all they can to suppress the testimonies of homosexuals who have changed. If it were accepted that homosexuals could change, "there would be no reason for people to continue to practice homosexuality, and all (homosexual) claims of 'goodness,' 'inevitability,' etc., would have to be rejected. The homosexual movement would come to a halt."[26]

When the American Psychiatric Association classified homosexuality as a disease, the real reason was not that they found it acceptable. It was because they couldn't cure it. The reason they couldn't cure it is simple: it is not a disease, it's a sin. Human devices alone are impotent against sin. Only the power of God, which is something psychiatrists seldom know about, can overcome it. But what a difference Christ's strength makes.

A homosexual testifies:

> A lot of people today say that it's impossible for a person with homosexual desires to be happy without living as an active homosexual. From my experience I can say that if it were not

for God, that would be true. But when I look at the life I have today, I can only thank God that it isn't true at all.[27]

Another says,

God saved me from a life that would have ended in misery. The stark facts of homosexual life began to stand out more clearly – the loneliness of one night stands, the fear of losing one's attractiveness, the hours spent in those pits of despair called gay bars. . . . It wasn't a matter of stifling my desires because of some arbitrary law. I just didn't want that life. I could look at it objectively and say, "That's not going to make me happy. That's going to kill me."[28]

Still another wonders,

When so many are asserting that homosexuality is a given – either you are or you aren't – how is it that my experience is so different? The Lord has shown me that my identity as a son of God was given to determine my life, to unravel all confusion about my identity as a man. Everything proceeds from the fact that I am a new creature in Christ. That truth is simple, but it makes all the difference in the world.[29]

HEALING FOR HOMOSEXUALS

Does God love homosexuals? The answer to that question is an unequivocal yes. He loves all of us the way we are, but when we become Christians, we become brand new persons inside (2 Cor. 5:17). You wouldn't say to an alcoholic, "God loves you, but he made you this way. Hence it's not the Church's job to change you but rather to help you learn to accept and rejoice in your drunkenness." The Bible nowhere condemns drinking, but it says that drunkenness will keep a person from inheriting God's kingdom (Gal. 5:19-21).

Similarly, the Lord is not against our enjoying sex. He is opposed to our becoming obsessed with it and exercising it in a destructive, unnatural way. Homosexual aberrations are abhorrent to God because he loves homosexuals. He doesn't want to see them miserable or, even worse, pushed into substance abuse or suicide by their own uncontrollable lusts.

Homosexuality is the ultimate example of man's vain attempts to achieve self-satisfaction apart from the purposes of God. It is the terrible expression of the counterproductivity of selfishness (Matt. 16:25), the triumph of fear over faith.

Hebrews 2:15 tells us that the fear of death leads us into slavery. That pertains to the fear of dying to self as well. The one who tries to save his or her life eventually loses it. With homosexuality we deal largely with people who are heterophobic. They fear the opposite sex and lack confidence in their ability to handle the tensions involved in relating to them. They are emotionally brutalized by the inner wounds of their past.

Seeking comfort and escape, homosexual men look for a partner who will gratify their insatiable craving for physical pleasure. Lesbians also seek a mate who will gratify their emotional hunger for intimacy. Both homosexual men and lesbians seek to avoid the "dying to self" that is an inevitable part of mature heterosexual married life. Both seek a refuge from their worst fear—the fear of rejection. This fear is intensified by the fact that they live contrary to their own nature while seeking to deny and anesthetize their guilt. The terrible, sad irony is that their life-style falls far short of being gay. One observer of the homosexual scene states, "While healthy heterosexual relationships are rich in tension and stimulating contrasts, homosexual relationships 'are overclose, fatigue-prone, and are often adjusted to narrow, trigger-sensitive tolerances. . . .' "[30]

Homosexuality is a particularly powerful bondage to break. It is more stubborn even than drug addiction because it infiltrates the fiber of one's character and identity. Many homosexuals pray for God to take away their evil desires, and when he doesn't, they conclude either that he made them that way or that he can't help them. Neither is true. No sins, especially those categorized as sins unto death, can be conquered so simplistically. The alcoholic, overeater, adulterer, or drug addict cannot get free from their bondage that easily, and the homosexual shouldn't expect to either. One homosexual spoke of a six-year struggle that gradually saw his orientation change from predominantly homosexual to predominantly heterosexual.[31]

SHOULD CHURCHES HELP?

A church should be actively equipping itself for ministry to homosexuals and other sexually disenfranchised people before it speaks out against their sins. We must help these desperate people find the healing they need. Legislative efforts to stem the tide of moral erosion are not enough to reverse society's self-destructive tendencies.

For most churches it takes a substantial commitment of life, resources, energy, and a veritable reorientation of their purpose and goals for them to become "hospitals for sinners." As with helping the victims of abortion, they will have to take Isaiah 58 seriously. Our vain religious rituals must be supplanted by sacrificial righteousness.

The fast that God speaks about in Isaiah 58:6-10 for his people far transcends the temporary denial of nutrition to enable us to bend God's ear to our desired petitions. He would have us "loosen the bonds of wickedness, to undo the bands of the yoke, and to let the oppressed go free, and break every yoke" (v. 6). We must "divide [our] bread with the hungry, . . . bring the homeless poor into the house" (v. 7) . . . and "remove the yoke from [our] midst, the pointing of the finger, and speaking wickedness" (v. 9). Those who give themselves to the hungry and satisfy the desire of the afflicted are promised astonishing rewards (vv. 10-14).

However, ministry to the homosexual involves more than inviting him to Sunday worship and Wednesday prayer meeting. Psalm 68:6 reminds us that "God makes a home for the lonely; He leads out the prisoners into prosperity. Only the rebellious dwell in a parched land." I am persuaded that the Lord establishes Christian homes so they can be used to restore and bring a health to those who have never known a happy home life and are emotionally scarred because of it. A megadose of healthy family living, where the homosexual sees God's love in action is one of the best antidotes to counteract his deficient family background.

Godly counsel is another important element. It is usually better if counselors have not been homosexuals themselves. Homosexuals need responsible counsel, firmly rooted in biblical absolutes and personally administered by counselors who through Christ have been victorious, having successfully waged war against their own sins. They should be willing to be available night or day to help the homosexual battle his.

Counselors should also be those who understand the implications of spiritual fatherhood (1 Cor. 4:14-21) and are willing to accept its responsibilities. Psalm 68:4 tells us that God is a father to the fatherless. The last verse of the Old Testament reminds us that the hearts of the fathers need to be restored to their children and the hearts of the children to their fathers or the earth will be cursed (Mal. 4:5-6). Homosexuality is but one of the manifestations of that curse on our culture.

How can fatherhood be restored and that curse arrested? James 1:27 tells us that true religion requires us to visit widows and orphans in their distress and keep ourselves unstained by the world. A literal understanding of that passage reveals that it is packed with profound implications for God's people. Anyone who has been raised by nonbelieving parents is a spiritual orphan (Col. 2:13). The word used for distress covers the whole gamut of afflictions, problems, and diseases fostered by a homosexual life-style. The word *visit* is one used to describe the manifest presence of Christ (as in "visitation of God") to bring judgment and/or restoration. True religion then means faithfully and tangibly representing Christ to people in desperate straits.

Charles Simpson once said that the purpose of spiritual authority is to represent the fatherhood of God. Spiritual orphans need to be responsibly fathered. It may be the only way to enable them to overcome their deficient family life. This concept is akin to the concept of reparenting discussed by psychiatrist M. Scott Peck.

> For the most part, mental illness is caused by an absence of or defect in the love that a particular child required from its particular parents for successful maturation and spiritual growth. It is obvious, then, that in order to be healed through psychotherapy the patient must receive from the psychotherapist at least a portion of the genuine love of which the patient was deprived. If the psychotherapist cannot genuinely love a patient, genuine healing will not occur. No matter how well credentialed and trained psychotherapists may be, if they cannot extend themselves through love to their patients, the results of their psychotherapeutic practice will be generally unsuccessful. Conversely, a totally uncredentialed and minimally trained lay therapist who exercises a great ca-

pacity to love will achieve psychotherapeutic results that
equal those of the very best psychiatrists.[32]

REPRESENTING GOD'S LOVE

It is my belief that, apart from Christ, the kind of love Peck
describes would be virtually impossible to give to another person.
Without God's Word it would be impossible even to define genuine
love; without his Spirit, it would be even more impossible to impart
it to another. Biblical love is patient, kind, not jealous, boastful or
arrogant; it does not seek selfish ends, is not easily provoked, over-
looks wrongs suffered; "bears all things, believes all things, hopes
all things, endures all things. Love never fails" (1 Cor. 13). Men find
such love is not easily attained, mainly because of sheer selfishness.
But this is exactly the kind of love people need to receive and learn
to give if they want to live a victorious Christian life.

What does it mean to represent the heavenly Father's love to another? The God of the Bible is not the permissive parent of human-
ism. He is merciful, to be sure, but his love also involves discipline
and is tough against those committing sins that would destroy
them. Without that, discipleship would be impossible, and apart
from authentic discipleship there is no power to overcome sin. The
author of Hebrews expresses it best. He begins by quoting from
Job and Proverbs, excellent places to look for wisdom for the be-
leaguered:

> "My son, do not regard lightly the discipline of the Lord. . . .
> For those whom the Lord loves He disciplines, and He
> scourges every son whom He receives." It is for discipline
> that you endure; God deals with you as with sons; for what
> son is there whom his father does not discipline? [Unfor-
> tunately, plenty today.] . . . Furthermore, we had earthly
> fathers to discipline us, and we respected them; shall we not
> much rather be subject to the Father of spirits, and live? For
> they disciplined us for a short time as seemed best to them,
> but He disciplines us for our good, that we may share His
> holiness. All discipline . . . yields the peaceful fruit of righ-
> teousness. (Heb. 12:5-11)

A person who would conquer such sins as homosexuality, adultery, and promiscuity will need more than being born again and filled with God's Spirit. He or she will even need more than spiritual deliverance (exorcism) and discipline, though all these things are probably necessary as well. They must make Jesus the Lord of their lives. Only then can the power of God become consistently available to overrule their weaknesses (2 Cor. 12:9) and perfect their sanctification (1 Thes. 5:23).

The Lord God told Israel that their sin was so great it was like an incurable wound (Jer. 30:12-15). He said, however, that he would restore the people to health and heal them of their wounds (v. 17). Jesus alluded to this need for inner healing when he said his mission included the release of captives (liberating people from their wounds) (Luke 4:18-19). Some sins cannot be overcome, some freedoms not obtained, until this profound inner healing takes place.

In fact, the cause of the Israelites' captivity by the Assyrians and Babylonians was directly related to this. Because the leaders of Israel failed to heal the diseased and bind up the broken, the people became religious instead of righteous and ended up being led into captivity by their enemies (Ezek. 34:1-16, 23-31). This captivity typified the bondage to sin from which Jesus came to liberate us (Matt. 1:21; John 8:31-36; 1 John 3:2-10).

This Jeremiah passage about captivity, of course, precedes chapter 31 which contains the blessed promises of the new covenant – a covenant between God and his people which is effectuated through a spiritual heart transplant. The heart is the seat of desire. A new heart is the promise of the new covenant (Jer. 31:31-34). Out of the heart flows all manner of evil (Mark 7:20-23), and the promised gift of a new heart most often cannot be obtained overnight.

A person must spiritually retrace the steps of the ancient Israelites on his own journey toward the kingdom of God, leaving behind the life of bondage, just as the Jews fled Egypt. That person probably will wander through the wilderness of indecision as he struggles against the desires of the flesh. Eventually he must fight the heart's idols and evil spirits that seek to keep him from inheriting a portion in the Land of Promise. At every step, victory is won in the battle for one's heart as he acknowledges that it is better to follow the Spirit than to indulge the flesh (Rom. 7-8).

I believe a godly counselor, one who is willing to faithfully represent the disciplinary love of God, can be a great source of wisdom, understanding, and strength on this kind of journey. For such counsel to be effective, it must be submitted to, as the Bible requires (Heb. 13:17). A doctor cannot help someone who refuses to take his ordered prescriptions. What is the use in going to a dentist and then refusing to let him work on your teeth? Pastoral counsel must likewise be respected, received, and acted upon.

This is not to encourage an unquestioning, blind obedience to a counselor. Feedback and communication are essential to any cure. A person who is seriously ill, however, may be more interested in avoiding pain than in dealing appropriately with his or her problems. This is true in the spiritual realm as well as in the natural.

There is help for the homosexual if he wants it badly enough. The importance of his getting it, both for himself and society, is underscored by these closing words from *The Institutes of Biblical Law:*

> Paul conceived of sin and its consequences as being in the closest possible connection: decay and death followed upon sin as inevitably as life and peace upon the righteousness of faith. . . . He sees the prevalence of homosexuality, the dishonoring of their bodies among themselves, as a manifestation not only of sin, but also of its issue and punishment, i.e., corruption and death.[33]
>
> The humanist rebels against God in order to exalt himself. The grim irony of judgment is that his act leads to dishonoring himself. The humanist seeks to glorify and honor his body, but he instead dishonors it openly and makes his disgrace a public fact.[34]
>
> Sex and religion are thus closely and inescapably linked in every nonbiblical faith. It is the religious result of apostasy: man worships his own sexual evil and exalts his disgrace into a way of life. Humanistic man worships "the moment" and converts "the spirit of transgression" into a religious principle. Such a faith cannot create or perpetuate a culture; it can only destroy it. Man must either rebuild in terms of the triune God or be plowed under by His judgment.[35]

202

NINETEEN
A POTPOURRI OF
DIFFICULT QUESTIONS
AND ANSWERS

There are numerous other areas of sexual activity we have yet to discuss. Some include quite serious offenses. Leviticus 20 condemns human sacrifice (which easily could describe abortion), homosexuality, and adultery, topics we have already considered as sins punishable by death. In addition, the New Testament lists certain other categories of sexual transgressions that keep a person from inheriting Christ's kingdom if he refuses to repent (1 Cor. 6:9-11; Gal. 5:16-25; Heb. 6:4-8; 10:26-31; Eph. 5:3-7; Rev. 21:7-8). Among those yet to be examined from Leviticus and the New Testament are incest, bigamy, bestiality, familial nudity, immorality, and sensuality. Given the seriousness with which the Bible judges these offenses, it goes without saying that the Christian must avoid them all.

Some other questions arise, however, relating to more ambiguous practices. There are certain gray areas of sexual activity to which we must turn our attention. These questions need to be responsibly addressed because they represent common problems that cause confusion among God's people as well as the world at large.

Q. *We have dealt with biblical absolutes, but what about gray areas? How should a Christian relate to questionable practices that are not specifically treated in the Scriptures?*

A. It is as important to be silent where the Bible is silent as it is to speak when the Bible speaks. The Church has deservedly lost a great deal of credibility by making absolutes out of things that are relative. Usually when Christians major in minors they don't even minor in majors. Jesus called this tendency among the Pharisees "straining out gnats" while they "swallow camels" (Matt. 23:24). This causes Christians to take stands on matters that are culturally related rather than on issues that are clearly condemned in the Scriptures. It involves valuing men's traditions more than God's commandments (Mark 7:7).

Much unnecessary confusion and condemnation results from this religiosity. Condemning things the Bible does not clearly prohibit can abnormally incite a person's desire for them, leading to much unnecessary frustration, guilt, and compulsion. As the Corinthians were told, "the power of sin is the law" (1 Cor. 15:56). Wrongfully applied, the law ministers bondage and death instead of life (Rom. 7:8–8:3).

Where the Bible is silent we are given some degree of latitude. Typical of this is Paul's statement in 1 Corinthians 6. Immediately after listing some biblical absolutes (vv. 9-10), he says:

> All things are lawful for me, but not all things are profitable. All things are lawful for me, but I will not be mastered by anything. Food is for the stomach, and the stomach is for food; but God will do away with both of them. Yet the body is not for immorality, but for the Lord; and the Lord is for the body. (1 Cor. 6:12-13)

God is not opposed to pleasure, but pleasure is not the purpose for which we were created, nor will it fulfill us. Paul recognized that "nothing is unclean in itself" (Rom. 14:14). "To the pure, all things are pure" (Titus 1:15). Jesus taught that men are not defiled by things that tempt them from without but by the evil they secretly harbor within (Mark 7:20-23). Paul established this guideline for his own personal choices, however. Though all *things* (notice he did not say all relationships) are lawful, he refused to indulge any desires he could not control. All sin leads to bondage (John 8:34-35).

Two other considerations guided his choices. First, he would do nothing that would cause another person to be offended (Rom. 14:1-15). "All things indeed are clean, but they are evil for the man who eats and gives offense" (v. 20). Also, "Whatever is not from faith is sin" (v. 23). He said, "The faith which you have, have as your own conviction before God. Happy is he who does not condemn himself in what he approves. But he who doubts is condemned if he eats, because his eating is not from faith" (vv. 22-23). A good way to remember these guidelines is the simple proverb, "When in doubt, do without." This will guard your conscience, and lead you to a happier life in the Lord.

Q. *What about oral sex? Doesn't the Bible condemn this practice?*

A. I put this question to a friend of mine years ago. He has been a pastor fifty years and is one of the holiest men I know. His answer floored me. He said, "Ken, nowhere does the Bible say that one part of your body is more unholy than any other. If you can kiss a person's lips why not their genitals?" Charlie Shedd, in his best-selling book, *Celebration in the Bedroom,* quotes a medical doctor who said, "Contrary to most people's understanding, the penis and vagina are not unsanitary. God made them clean and healthy. In most cases it is the mouth where the germs are."[1]

Shedd then offers us these liberating guidelines:

In our tuning in to the living Word, this is the message:

"Anything you both want to do
Anything you both enjoy
Anything not physically, mentally, nor psychologically harmful
Anything not forbidden in my Book
Is excellent in every way."[2]

This, in fact, may be the true meaning of the Scripture so often misapplied: "Let the marriage bed be undefiled" (Heb. 13:4).

If you can shed your cultural inhibitions and care more about your mate's sexual needs than about our own, what is right will not be hard to discern. Prayer, communication, and understanding will carry a couple a long way. Nothing that would make your mate feel uncomfortable should ever be forced on him or her, however. And never withhold sex except by mutual agreement for a time that you may devote yourselves to prayer (1 Cor. 7:5). With God's help you can have a marriage abounding with joyful offerings of genuine love that brings fulfillment and blessing.

Q. *What about anal intercourse? Isn't this what the Bible condemns as sodomy?*

A. Again, may I lean on the Shedds? Their answer to this question is balanced, sensitive, and concise:

> Bible scholars disagree on the definition of sodomy. A few might say it includes anal intercourse, but most believe it deals exclusively with homosexuality.
>
> Conclusion: Say it again—When the Bible is not specific, it is up to each of us to decide before God what is right for us.[3]

Recent publications warn of the dangers of anal sex. Dr. Woodrow Myers, a critical-care physician at the San Francisco General Hospital Medical Center says: "There is no safe homosexual anal sex. There are a number of medical complications of anal intercourse that can lead, even with treatment, to serious disability or death."[4]

Given our developing information on the transmission of Acquired Immune Deficiency Syndrome (AIDS) through anal intercourse, I sincerely recommend that any married couple engaging in this practice be as clean as possible. Condoms should be used at all times, and couples must be careful that their hands are clean. We know too little about how the AIDS virus is transmitted to feel safe about unprotected anal intercourse, even for monogamous married couples.

Q. *What about pornography? Are R-rated movies OK? How about X-rated? Where do you draw the line?*

A. The word *pornography* comes from the Greek word *porne*, or *prostitute*, and *graph*, meaning "pictures and drawings." It literally means "immoral pictures or drawings." Since sensuality and immorality can keep a person from inheriting Christ's kingdom (Gal. 5:19-21), and the Bible reminds us that "lust of the eyes" is an insatiable part of the world that is passing away (1 John 2:15-17), we need to be careful. Impurity keeps a person from inheriting God's kingdom (Eph. 5:3-5). Impurity describes any moral "uncleanness that clings like infection and renders (us) unserviceable" or "excludes (us) from fellowship with God."[5] We are warned to "flee from youthful lusts" (2 Tim. 2:22) and "make no provision for the lusts of the flesh" (Rom. 13:14). If our eye offends us we are to pluck it out (Matt. 5:28-29), so severe is the possibility of being cast into hell through adultery in our hearts. Anything that causes uncontrollable lust or causes another to stumble is sinful. In light of this it is wise to avoid explicit pornographic films.

Q. *What about pornographic magazines? Is the portrayal of nudity acceptable if it is tastefully done? Can't it be artistic?*

A. We have been awash in pornography since the "experts," under President Richard Nixon's administration, assured us that it was harmless. The penalty which society has paid for their bizarre misjudgment is far greater than anything Watergate did to us as a nation. The effect this has had on our divorce rate, abortion statistics, increase in suicides, rapes, sexual abuse of children, homosexuality, venereal disease, and just plain problems in all areas of relationships between men and women is staggering. Since the fall of man and the shame that inevitably accompanied it, the Lord has recognized and taught that nudity is a private matter between a man and his wife (Lev. 18:5-8). Beyond that context problems are inevitable.

The National Federation for Decency reports that 77 percent of child molesters of boys, and 87 percent of child molesters of girls admitted imitating the sexual behavior they had seen modeled in pornography. Adult pornography is a doorway to child pornography. Pedophiles almost always begin with adult pornography. They furthermore report that since obscenity laws were relaxed in the early 1960s, reported rapes are up 116 percent and commercial vice has increased 80 percent.

Why is nudity such a big issue? I personally believe that our society's obsession with women's breasts stems largely from the trend in the forties and fifties away from breast feeding. This has caused an unrequired need for nurturance in both men and women. Those advertisers, pornographers, and nude models who plunder that need for their own profit will someday stand before God and acknowledge the multitudes that have been forced to suffer because of their irresponsibility. When that happens all protestations of ignorance and rationalizations in their own defense will be meaningless, for they instinctively know their own shame. They have ignored their conscience's attempts to warn them.

Pornographic magazines have harmed the lives of multitudes of people. Christians should refuse to patronize all convenience marts, drugstores, and supermarkets that carry such products. Our dollars can make a difference. We may not be able to keep the world from destroying itself, but we ought not to subsidize its moral suicide. I have been involved with the Northern Ohio Roundtable's efforts that recently helped drive pornography out of many drug and convenience chains across the nation. Christians are a potent economic and political force in our nation. Uniting and focusing our energies can make a substantial difference.

Q. *What about masturbation? Isn't this what the Bible calls Onanism?*

A. The phrase Onanism refers to a passage found in Genesis 38:4, 8-10. In this passage Onan's brother died leaving his wife childless. Under Deuteronomic law Onan had an obligation to marry her so that the family line would continue. Because he knew that the child would not be called his, Onan "wasted his seed on the ground, in order not to give offspring to his brother" (v. 9). What he did displeased the Lord and so he took Onan's life. It's important to note, however, that the Lord was displeased by Onan's attempt to defraud his sister-in-law and disregard the Deuteronomic code, not by the act of wasting his seed on the ground.

Another phrase sometimes used to categorically condemn masturbation is the vague prohibition against "abusers of themselves with mankind" (1 Cor. 6:9, KJV). There is no agreement among Bible teachers as to the actual meaning of this phrase, however. It cannot be used as a definitive statement against masturbation since the phrase specifically refers to something done with others, and masturbation is a solo attempt at sexual arousal.

Having said that, I must caution against encouraging unmarried young people to masturbate as a "harmless" release of sexual tension. First of all, it would probably be impossible to so stimulate oneself without indulging lust in one's heart (Matt. 5:27, 28). Second, the guilt and reduced self-esteem this practice causes only compounds a person's adjustment to his or her sexuality. Third, the fantasizing that masturbation requires creates a false understanding of sexual relationships and can make marital adjustments more difficult. Finally, masturbation does not encourage the self-control that is essential to a relationship even after marriage. It is perhaps the ultimate act of selfishness with few if any redeeming benefits.

Yet masturbation of itself is not a sin unto death. Though it can lead to a confused thought life, low self-image, and a distorted view of reality, it could be a lesser evil in some instances. A businessman on a prolonged trip could conceivably reduce his vulnerability to temptation by masturbating while fantasizing about his wife. Masturbation, however, can easily become a serious bondage that injects guilt, frustration, a sense of alienation, and self-condemnation into a relationship. It should be practiced only with the utmost care and caution.

Q. *Isn't prostitution a victimless crime? Shouldn't we favor its legalization as a means of preventing the spread of disease and providing harmless sexual release for those who otherwise wouldn't have it?*

A. There is no such thing as a victimless crime or a harmless sin. The Bible clearly teaches that he who joins himself to a harlot becomes one with her and thereby prostitutes his own relationship with God (1 Cor. 6:15-20). In addition, there is the harm done to the prostitutes themselves. In exposing their sexuality to various men they not only endanger their bodies but their personalities as well. Certainly vulnerable, teenage runaways are cruelly victimized by their pimps. Even those who pay for prostitutes are victims. They receive a shallow and shabby substitute for the real love they crave that can only be found within the bounds of marriage.

Naive, religious bureaucrats who support the legalization of prostitution as their latest "higher moral cause" should be removed from positions of ecclesiastical authority. Bible-believing Christians should leave any denomination that would refuse to root out such evildoers from their midst.

Q. *What about birth control?*

A. There is nothing in the Bible prohibiting birth control. No person, however, should use it if it violates his or her conscience or the teachings of that person's church. Some churches consider the use of birth control to be sinful. For sincere Christians the issue of spiritual authority is so important (the Bible clearly teaches submission to spiritual authority) that, if they belong to such a church, they need to honor their church's teachings (Heb. 13:17 and elsewhere). If they cannot in good conscience do this, they ought to find another church whose teachings and authority they can wholeheartedly embrace.

Christians should know that IUDs (intrauterine devices) and some birth control pills can cause serious health problems as well as induce abortions and hence should not be used.[6] Men and women should carefully explore their alternatives in these areas before making any decisions regarding different types of birth control or surgery.

Q. *What about the differences in the sexual needs of men and women? How can a husband and wife achieve compatibility?*

A. Probably the classic statement of this problem was made in a Woody Allen film. On a split screen it showed a husband and wife each privately conferring with their separate psychiatrists. The husband was complaining that his wife was frigid. His evidence? She refused to have sex with him more than three times a week. Simultaneously the wife was accusing her husband of being obsessed with sex. Her proof? He desired intercourse three times a week!

Few problems are brought to me with greater frequency than this one. The wife usually complains about her husband's emotional inaccessibility while the husband decries his wife's sexual unavailability. The problem belies a fundamental misunderstanding on the part of men and women. Most women don't require sex as often as their husbands (though sometimes the opposite is true). Most men don't desire as much communication from their wives as their wives would appreciate from them. Unresolved, this dilemma may cause either or both partners to seek someone outside their relationship for understanding that they should be able to get from their mate.

If a man wants sex more frequently with his wife, he had better be prepared to give her his ears. If a wife wants her husband's heart, she'll need to reach him through other avenues besides his stomach, though that helps too! A Christian couple, committed to God and one another, can transform their temporary incompatibility into an opportunity for their own growth in selflessness. Each partner needs to learn to give, communicate, and sacrifice expectations in new and blessed ways. The benefits of loving sacrificially far outweigh the cost.

Q. *What is a sadomasochist? How can such a person be helped?*

A. Sadism gets its name from the late Marquis de Sade, whose writings described various sexual aberrations. It refers to the practice of "getting sexual pleasure from dominating, mistreating, or hurting one's partner physically or otherwise."[7]

Masochism is named after Leopold von Sacher-Mosach. It

refers, conversely, to the practice of "getting sexual pleasure from being dominated, mistreated, or hurt physically or otherwise by one's partner."[8] Often the practices are linked together, hence the term sadomasochism (S/M). (Could this be the real meaning of the biblical phrase, "abusers of themselves with mankind"?) This aberration is a dangerous and humiliating perversion of biblical order and sexual expression. It is usually embraced by confused people for whom pleasure has become an end in itself. Withdrawn from the context of a permanently committed relationship, illicit sexual pleasure eventually becomes uninteresting. Without the growing emotional, relational, and spiritual dynamics of a healthy marriage, our appetites become dull, our tastes increasingly jaded. Paradoxically, for some emotionally ill individuals pain becomes a requisite for pleasure.

I am further convinced that the sadomasochist is subconsciously aware of his need to be punished for his illicit sexuality. He may also be seeking to inflict punishment on others who have become symbols of his own temptation, inner anguish, and sin. The pain, in some twisted way, temporarily atones for his transgressions, releasing him again to momentarily enjoy pleasure.

Similarly the person who enjoys cruel domination, bondage, and submission perversely expresses the valid need for godly order and authority. He or she may never have known the comfort of having parents who cared enough to administer the loving discipline and training so essential to having a blessed and self-disciplined life.

These practices have become so warped as to lead to a new pornographic thrill: snuff films. These are movies in which people are actually killed at the moment of orgasm—all the while, the cameras are relentlessly rolling. These films are the ultimate example of the misguided union of *thanatos* and *eros*, death and love.

Even a person with such bizarre appetites for pain can through godly counsel and discipline be restored to a place of genuine freedom. Without such help these people's lives unavoidably plunge toward greater emptiness, depression, despair, aberration, and ultimately death.

Q. *Should abortion be justified for victims of rape and incest? Couldn't this be a righteous way to keep a person from suffering more?*

A. No one who understands the harm abortions cause or the biblical basis for a pro-life ethic could ever think so. A developing child who is a product of rape or incest is no less an innocent human life than any other unborn baby. We are no more justified in handing him the death sentence for his father's sins than we would be if he were conceived from a voluntary act of sexual intercourse. Evangelicals who would ideologically sacrifice these harmless innocents to the abortionists' devices have unwittingly forsaken the very foundation of a biblical life ethic. The same is true for those who consider the retarded or deformed to be less the divine image-bearers than so-called normal people.

If for no other reason than an informed view of the consequences of abortion, however, Christians must reject this pseudosolution to the terrible problem of rape and incest. A woman is never better off having an abortion rather than a baby. Medical and psychological complications as well as the risk of suicidal despair and infertility all render abortion immeasurably more harmful than childbirth. Those who say otherwise are either lying or ignorant of the medical facts. If we truly care for the victim of rape and incest, we dare not prescribe abortion for them.

Q. *Does the Bible say anything about AIDS or other deadly venereal diseases?*

A. The passage from Romans 1 discussed in the chapter on homosexuality reminds us that homosexuals receive "in their own persons the due penalty of their error" (v. 27). AIDS and other such diseases may be the natural expression of that penalty. God doesn't afflict these people; nature itself does as a result of unnatural practices.

In seeking to find a solution for this awful problem, however, another Scripture intrigues me. It tells us that pleasure, or passion, is "rottenness to the bones" (Prov. 14:30). The homosexual life-style idolizes pleasure. Is it possible that this causes a chemical effect on the bone marrow that prevents it from making the kind of blood that builds up a person's immune system? It would take a good deal of medical research to either verify or refute this possibility. (It is interesting to note that since these words were penned, secular scientists have begun to explore bone transplants as a possible solution to the AIDS disease.)

It is entirely possible that Christian doctors searching the Scriptures for medical clues might come up with the same kind of medical breakthroughs that occurred when the wisdom of biblical cleanliness was applied to medicine in the nineteenth century. In that era a frightening number of women were dying as a result of pregnancy and childbirth. Up to that time medical doctors were unaware of the possibilities of infection because of unwashed hands. They routinely went from treating one disease to another, often examining their female patients without prior washings. The doctor who first suggested that biblical patterns of cleanliness and washing could be significant in stopping these unwanted deaths was scorned and ostracized. Even though he was able to dramatically reduce these unnecessary deaths through cleanliness, the medical establishment was slow to embrace his procedures. For years many people continued to die needlessly because of the medical community's unwillingness to heed the clear and simple wisdom of the Bible.[9]

The same ostracism probably awaits Christian physicians, psychologists, behavioral scientists, and social workers, not to mention pastors and sexologists who attempt to return people to the sane simplicity of biblical wisdom. They will help many while simultaneously being scorned by the dogmatic and deceived humanists who control our medical schools, universities, seminaries, and mainline religious bureaucracies.

CONCLUSIONS FOR LIFE

The wisdom of the Scriptures is eternal, unchanging and relentless in its exposure of folly. Through it

> "the glory of the Lord will be revealed, and all flesh will see it together; for the mouth of the Lord has spoken." . . . All flesh is grass, and all its loveliness is like the flower of the field. . . . The grass withers, the flower fades, but the word of our God stands forever. (Isa. 40:5-8)

That eternal Word is as relevant today as it was two thousand or four thousand years ago.

Our Lord easily could have had our modern psychological and

sexological experts in mind when he contrasted worldly wisdom with that which is truly spiritual:

> For it is written, "I will destroy the wisdom of the wise, and the cleverness of the clever I will set aside." Where is the wise man? Where is the scribe? Where is the debater of this age? Has not God made foolish the wisdom of the world? (1 Cor. 1:19-20)

Paul goes on to remind Christians:

> Now we have received, not the spirit of the world, but the Spirit who is from God, that we might know the things freely given to us by God, which things we also speak, not in words taught by human wisdom, but in those taught by the Spirit, combining spiritual thoughts with spiritual words. But a natural man does not accept the things of the Spirit of God; for they are foolishness to him, and he cannot understand them, because they are spiritually appraised. But he who is spiritual appraises all things, yet he himself is appraised by no man. For who has known the mind of the Lord, that he should instruct him? But we have the mind of Christ. (1 Cor. 2:12-16)

He finally cautions us:

> Let no man deceive himself. If any man among you thinks that he is wise in this age, let him become foolish that he may become wise. For the wisdom of this world is foolishness before God. For it is written, "*He is* the One who catches the wise in their craftiness"; and again, "The Lord knows the reasonings of the wise, that they are useless." (1 Cor. 3:18-20)

Useless and sadly counterproductive. This world, for all its crass openness about sex, for all its vaunted new morality, sexology, pseudoliberation and allegedly superior moral principles is plunging even deeper into frustration, unfulfillment, and moral chaos. If Christians can rediscover the simple but profound joy our loving Creator built into creation, and learn to live it before the world, we may yet be able to call back our society from its moral precipice. We may lead it out of its darkness and into a new day of genuine freedom and delight. If we fail to embrace the Lord's purposes for ourselves, we will probably perish along with the world. That terrible choice will always be ours.

But thank God we have a choice. It is the Lord's gift of grace that those who obey him are rewarded in full. And because his earthly design for us is one of order—a reflection of his own nature—we find total fulfillment in obedience to him.

Sex, then, becomes most pleasurable when sought and consummated according to the rules God laid out for us. It is a wondrous and beautiful gift, from the Lord and the wellspring of life itself. Utmost intimacy involves the surrender of one's total being, and embodies God's eternal design as well: self-sacrifice. Those who would know the wonders of sex will keep that in mind—that this beautiful gift is but a segment of his greatest gift—love.

TWENTY
SHOULD WE
LEGISLATE MORALITY?
AN IMPORTANT
POLITICAL POSTSCRIPT

The mistaken assumption that you cannot legislate morality has dominated our state and federal legislatures in recent years. However, most legislation is in fact a codification of values and standards. Morality, after all, is nothing more than instruction in right and wrong conduct. Since the law is a potent teacher, all laws – in varying degrees – legislate morality. The question is not whether we can legislate morality but whose morality we will legislate. Shall we embrace our Judeo-Christian heritage or capitulate to the naive and unproven premises of our modern-day utopian social architects?

If we care about individuals and civilization, we must restore our society to a biblical legal foundation. It was the righteous wisdom of the Scriptures that enabled us to become the most powerful and prosperous nation in history. Should we reject these scriptural precepts, we will reap the social disintegration and other problems that are the inevitable consequences of decadence.

It would be enlightening to discover to what degree our federal deficit is a by-product of the sexual revolution. Sin most certainly spawns poverty. I have been told as much as 90 percent of our welfare budget in some areas supports the victims of broken homes.

Specific examples abound. The relaxation of our divorce laws, coupled with the erosion of our social concensus against premarital sex, has plunged millions of women and their dependent children into poverty. How much money would our governments save on welfare, Aid to Dependent Children (ADC), Medicare payments, counseling services, suicide prevention programs and a host of other inadequate, stop-gap measures if we again reinforced the sanctity and permanence of marriage, affirmed the value of sexual responsibility, and refused to subsidize divorce and immorality? The government can not free people to make wise choices, but it need not pay for and thus encourage their foolish ones. The more important issue is how much unnecessary human misery could be averted if our laws affirmed traditional values.

How much money will AIDS cost us? More important, how many precious lives will it squander? It is estimated that soon one in ten people in America will have been exposed to the disease. The attempts to render homosexuality acceptable precipitated this dreaded plague. Only a return to biblical values can staunch it. Will we find politicians and clergy with the moral resolve to reverse the tendencies encouraged by a greedy and manipulated media elite acting on a perverse sense of misplaced compassion? If we do, a lot of people won't have to die, and much needless agony can be avoided.

What about the proliferation of pain resulting from pornography? At least one in four women and an increasing number of men are growing up as victims of rape, incest, and childhood sexual abuse. Yet we let our drugstores and convenience stores become purveyors of the very perversion that plants the degenerate seeds for these assaults into the hearts of weak-willed, vulnerable men and boys. What price must we pay in the lives of kidnapped children and abused infants before we realize the awful cost of lust?

Similar statements could be made about the harm abortion does to women, the torturous dismembering of families through adultery, and other violations of biblical morality. It is easy to see why moral decadence eventually destroys great and mighty civilizations. The wages of sin are obviously insufficient when compared to its exhorbitant price tag.

What can be done? I used to believe that a revival of true religion was enough. Though I am still convinced that nothing less than a profound spiritual renewel can turn our country around, I also now realize that unless that revival impacts the moral and legal foundations of our nation, its effects will be woefully short-lived and thoroughly insufficient to the enormous task of regenerating society. The truth of the matter is this: No one can be forced into being moral through legislation. If a person is intent upon sinning, there is no law written that can guarantee he will stop. However, the law is not ineffectual. If it were, so many radical liberal groups wouldn't work so hard to change it.

Righteous laws can foster a positive social environment, one that enables peer group pressure to influence the choices of the individual. Unrighteous laws can have an equally negative effect. Along with unwise government policies, they can actually encourage foolish choices. (The Bible labels as folly any behavior that is against the best interests of the person committing it.) They can keep people from realizing the full consequences of making the same mistake two, or three, or a dozen times. (I am told the *average* Soviet woman has six abortions.)

As Charles Simpson says, social problems are family problems that never got solved. There are never going to be sufficient resources for the government to take the place of responsible family behavior. Those who are seduced by this reasoning will find themselves becoming bedfellows with a government that strongly resembles Big Brother.

We not only need an undergirding of our laws against immoral behavior, but we also need government policies that refuse to reward self-destructive sin. If a girl sees pregnancy as a way out of the home, she will be tempted to try it. If the only way a woman gets more money is through having more children, what do you think she will do? If young boys can continue to impregnate teenage girls and get away with a three-hundred-dollar abortion, why shouldn't they? If husbands can leave their wives and children and count on the government to support them, won't they do just that when being responsible becomes burdensome and temptation comes knocking? If women can find a government-sponsored day-care center to provide for their infant children why should they stay home? Unfortunately much of society makes them feel foolish and somehow substandard for fulfilling that difficult and important role of full-time mother to their young children.

To address each of these concerns we need creative laws and policies like the one recently enacted in one of the state legislatures. Pro-life and pro-choice activists joined hands, for perhaps the first time in history, to support a law that is seeking to get to the root of the problem of unwanted pregnancy. It makes the parents of teenagers financially responsible for the offspring of their unmarried children. Laws and policies like that can become a part of the solution instead of a contributing factor to the problem.

We need lawmakers who will sponsor and support scripturally moral legislation. This is not the coercion of a minority religious opinion, it is a return to the values and standards that made us a happy and prosperous people. Biblical Christians have as much right as agnostic humanists to advance their moral standards. This is not government establishment of a religion, it is a constitutionally guaranteed free exercise of our religious beliefs. Most of our two-hundred-year history bears this out. Biblical values reigned supreme throughout our history and were never misinterpreted to be an unlawful establishment of religion. Apart from the responsible constraints of biblical values, freedom cannot long endure. It quickly degenerates into licentiousness that can only be restrained through some sort of fascist suppression.

Those who advocate biblical legal reforms will need courage. There will be detractors in the media and society who slander such efforts, labeling them archaic and even demagogic. Prophets and those who acted on their behalf in the Bible met with similar resistance. Those who care more about men's approval than the Lord's will not take such risks. But those who stand for God will eventually have the approval of both.

Who says you can't legislate morality? It's a ridiculous position to defend. Should we dismantle our laws against stealing, rape, murder, and child abuse? These are all predicated on moral values. Ultimately all legislation is based on moral values – standards of right and wrong.

Few things in life hold the power over us as does our sexuality; nothing needs more wise and careful oversight and government. Immorality, not Mongol hordes, are the bane of history's great free societies. Those who would ignore the past would doom us to learning the hard way some of history's most painful and devastating lessons. In this life as well as the next, they will live to regret their folly.

APPENDIX: ORGANIZATIONS ADVOCATING A BIBLICAL APPROACH TO SEXUALITY

The following is a partial list of organizations involved in advocating a biblical view of sexuality and assisting people in need in a scriptural way. These are the organizations which we are aware of at this time. We encourage you to support their efforts and write them directly for more information.

Help for Homosexuals

1. *Karatana,* 1734 Huntington Turnpike, Trumbull, CT 06611. Information on a Christian therapeutic approach to the healing and deliverance of homosexuals.

2. *Love in Action,* Box 2655, San Rafael, CA 95902. Former homosexuals committed to helping homosexuals to freedom in Christ. Excellent literature available.

3. *The Overcomers,* Box 925, Flint, MI 48501. Information, literature, and assistance for counselors desiring to help homosexuals and support those who have found a new life in Christ.

Pro-Life Organizations

1. *Alternatives to Abortion International,* c/o Pregnancy Distress Center, 999 South High Street, Columbus, OH 43206. Dedicated to developing centers and ministries to offer alternatives to abortion to women faced with unwanted pregnancies.

2. *Christian Action Council,* 422 C Street N.E., Washington, D.C. 20002. A Christ-centered approach to getting biblical Christians involved in the fight for life. Also an exceptional network to start, support, and assist crisis pregnancy centers.

3. *Intercessors for America* (and International), P. O. Box 2639, Reston, VA 22090. Network of Christians around the world committed to praying for the restoration of godly values. Excellent pro-life brochures available.

4. *National Right to Life Committee,* Suite 402, 419 7th Street N.W., Washington, D.C. 20004. The major political arm of the right to life movement. This excellent organization has significant offices in all major cities and state capitals.

5. *Pro-Life Non-Violent Action Project*, P. O. Box 2193, Gaithers-burg, MD 20879.
   An activist arm of the pro-life movement, committed to direct action as a means of saving the unborn and closing abortion chambers.
6. *Pro-Life Protestants*, Box 214, Kingsville, OH 44048.
   Dedicated to getting Christians of all varieties committed to the right to life. This group has excellent materials on abortion and premarital sex.

Pro-Family Organizations

1. *Concerned Women for America*, 122 C Street N.W., Suite 800, Washington, D.C. 20001.
   With a membership many times larger than NOW's, this competent women's organization stands for a biblical posture on issues related to women and families.
2. *Eagle Forum*, Alton, IL 62002.
   This dedicated cadre of committed Christians is a powerful force for Christian values—headed by Phyllis Schlafly.
3. *Focus on the Family*, P. O. Box 500, Arcadia, CA 91006-0500.
   Dr. James Dobson's potent radio and publication ministry offers solid, godly leadership to millions.
4. *Liberty Foundation*, Lynchburg, VA 24506
   Truly the humanists favorite scapegoat, this powerful grass roots ministry, founded by Jerry Falwell, has been a significant factor in presenting Christian views to our nation's political structures.
5. *National Federation for Decency*, P. O. Drawer 2440, Tupelo, MS 38803.
   A leading organization in the fight against pornography and discrimination against biblical Christians in the media. They produce a fine, informative magazine uniting Christians to boycott the sponsors of morally questionable products and services.
6. *One Life Ministries*, Box 214, Kingsville, OH 44048.
   Dedicated to the belief that one life, your life, can make a difference. This organization is developing a grass roots strategy for making Christians a significant economic and political force in their communities.
7. *The Rutherford Institute*, P. O. Box 510, Manassas, VA 22110.
   A Christian alternative to the ACLU, this legal arm of the biblical Christian community fights unselfishly for many causes with which we are in sympathy.

NOTES

CHAPTER 1.–*Search for Utopia*
1. Rollo May, *Love and Will* (New York: Dell, 1974 [1969]), 39.
2. C. Safran, "Why Religious Women Are Good Lovers," *Redbook*, April 1976, 155.

CHAPTER 3.–*Laws and the Gift of Guilt*
1. Abraham H. Maslow, *Religions, Values and Peak Experiences* (New York: Viking, 1970 [1964]), x.
2. Harris R. Laird, Gleason L. Archer, Jr., and Bruce K. Waltke, eds., *Theological Wordbook of the Old Testament* (Chicago: Moody Press, 1980), I, 349.
3. Ibid, II, 976-77.

CHAPTER 4.–*Immorality: Inner Emptiness with No Boundaries*
1. Henri Nouwen, *The Wounded Healer* (Garden City, N.Y.: Image Books, 1979), 3-4.
2. Herman Hesse, *Steppenwolf* (New York: Holt, Rinehart and Winston, 1961 [1929]), 22.
3. Kahlil Gibran, *The Prophet* (New York: Alfred A. Knopf, 1972 [1923]), 60.

CHAPTER 5.–*Israel and America: Parallel Lands of Promise*
1. John Powell, *Unconditional Love* (Niles, Ill.: Argus Communications, 1978), 7-8.

CHAPTER 6.–*Freudian Fallacies*
1. May, 70, n. 5.
2. Ibid.
3. Herbert Marcuse, *Eros and Civilization*, 2nd ed. (New York: Random House, 1962), 3.
4. Randy Frame, "Sex without Love," *Christianity Today*, April 22, 1983, 25.
5. May, 84.
6. Ibid.
7. Ibid, 85.
8. Ibid, 71-72.
9. Ibid, 73.

10. Ibid, 82.
11. Henri Nouwen, *Clowning in Rome* (Garden City, N.Y.: Image Books, 1979), 41.

CHAPTER 7.—*The Divine Design*
1. May, 39.
2. Mildred Bangs Wynkoop, *A Theology of Love* (Kansas City, Mo.: Beacon Hill Press, 1972), 120.
3. Victor Paul Furnish, *The Love Command in the New Testament* (Nashville: Abingdon Press, 1972), 90.

CHAPTER 8.—*False Freedom*
1. Source unknown.
2. Gibran, 47-48.
3. The document Declaration of Feminism.
4. *Women's Liberation: Notes from the Second Year.*

CHAPTER 9.—*The Marvelous One-Flesh Mystery*
1. Everett F. Harrison, ed., *Baker's Dictionary of Theology* (Grand Rapids: Baker Books, 1973), 223.
2. A. J. Russel, ed., *God Calling* (Old Tappan, N.J.: Spire Books, 1974), 25-26.

CHAPTER 10.—*The School of Sacrifice*
1. Also see "Love: The Most Important Ingredient in Happiness" by R. M. Gordon, *Psychology Today*, July 1976, 98.
2. Henry Drummond, *The Greatest Thing in the World* (London and Glasgow: Collins [Greetings Books]), 40.
3. *Webster's New World Dictionary*, College Edition (Cleveland and New York: The World Publishing Company, 1966), 576.

CHAPTER 11.—*Sexual Differences and Their Significance: The Solution for Loneliness*
1. Steven Goldberg, *The Inevitability of Patriarchy* (New York: William Morrow, 1973), 49.
2. Ibid, 51.
3. Taylor Caldwell, *Dear and Glorious Physician* (New York: Bantam, 1962), 425-426.
4. John B. Noss, *Man's Religions* (New York and London: McMillan and Collier, 1974), 242.
5. Ibid.
6. Ibid.

7. Margaret Mead, *Male and Female* (New York: William Morrow, 1984).
8. Melvin Konner, "He and She," *Science '82*, September, 56.
9. Ibid.
10. Ibid.
11. Ibid, 57.
12. Ibid, 61.
13. Paul Vitz, "Husbands, Love Your Wives," *Pastoral Renewal*, 8, No. 4, November 1983, 47-48.
14. Michael Novak, "The Sex of Christmas," *National Review*, 23 December 1983, 1616.
15. Ashley Montagu, "A 'Kinsey Report' on Homosexualities," *Psychology Today*, August 1978, 65.
16. Don Williams, *The Bond That Breaks: Will Homosexuality Split the Church?* (Los Angeles: BIM, Inc., 1978), 34, n. 70.; quoting C. A. Tripp, *The Homosexual Matrix* (New York: Signet Books, 1976), 157.
17. Powell, 92-93.

CHAPTER 12.—*Feminism's Fatal Flaws*

1. Quoted by Elisabeth Elliot, *Let Me Be a Woman* (Wheaton, Ill.: Tyndale House, 1976), 158.
2. Allan Carlson, "The Androgyny Hoax," *Persuasion at Work*, 9, No. 3, 2; quoting Ferdinand Lundberg and Marynia F. Farnham, M.D., *Modern Woman: The Lost Sex* (New York: Harper and Brothers, 1947), 92, 162-7, 353-76.
3. As documented in a White Paper I authored several years ago, mainline church bureaucracies have championed feminist values, abortion on demand, and homosexual rights. One United Methodist church in San Francisco even sponsored the making of explicit pornographic movies.
4. Carlson, quoting Shulamith Firestone, *The Dialectic of Sex: The Case for Feminist Revolution* (New York: William Morrow, 1970), 233-240, 272.
5. The document Declaration of Feminism.
6. George Gilder, *Sexual Suicide* (New York: Quadrangle, 1973).
7. Carlson, quoting Ann Ferguson, "Androgyny as an Ideal for Human Development (1974)," in *Feminism and Philosophy*, Mary Vetterling-Braggin, Frederick A. Elliston, and Jane English, eds. (Totowa, N.J.: Rowman and Littlefield, 1977), 45-69.
8. Ibid, quoting Edward A. Tiryakian, "Sexual Anomie, Social Structure, Societal Change," *Social Focus 59* (1981): 1026-1053.

9. Vitz, 47.
10. Carlson, quoting Firestone.
11. Ibid, quoting Andrea Dworkin, *Woman Hating* (New York: E. P. Dutton, 1974), 174-193.
12. Dorothy R. Pape, *In Search of God's Ideal Woman* (Downers Grove, Ill.: InterVarsity Press, 1976), 25.
13. Ibid. 24.
14. See Larry Christenson, *The Christian Family* (Minneapolis: Bethany Fellowship, 1970), for a biblical explanation of submission.
15. Christenson, 135-36.
16. Vitz, 47.
17. The Methodist Wedding Ritual in *The Cokesbury Marriage Manual* (New York and Nashville: Abingdon Press, 1961), 25.

CHAPTER 13.—*Spiritual Authority and Social Renewal*
1. Bob Mumford, *Focusing on Present Issues* (Life Changers, 6301 Pembroke Rd., Hollywood, FL 33023, 1979).

CHAPTER 14.—*Broken Covenants, Broken People: The Question of Divorce and Remarriage*
1. See Derek Prince, *The Marriage Covenant* (Fort Lauderdale: Derek Prince Ministries, 1982) for a full elaboration on this theme.
2. *Matthew Henry* (Wilmington, Del.: Sovereign Grace Publishers, 1972), II, 36.
3. Friedrich, Gerhard, eds., *Kittel's Theological Dictionary of the New Testament (TDNT)* (Grand Rapids: William B. Eerdmans, 1964), VI, 580.
4. Ibid, 591.
5. Ibid, 592.
6. Erlanger, ed., *Luther's Werke*, 51, 37, as quoted in Christenson, 25.
7. *TDNT,* II, 60.
8. Ibid, 261.
9. Ibid, 279.
10. Robert and Alice Fryling, *A Handbook for Engaged Couples* (Downers Grove, Ill.: InterVarsity Press, 1977).

CHAPTER 15.—*The Horse without the Carriage: What's Wrong with Premarital Sex?*
1. The *Cleveland Plain-Dealer Sunday* Magazine, 30 November 1982.

2. James H. Ford, M.D., and Michael Schwartz, "Birth Control for Teenagers: Diagram for Disaster," *Linacre Quarterly*, 46, No. 1, 73-74; reprinted in an expose of Planned Parenthood by S. and R. Glasgow, Human Life Education Fund, Altoona, Pa.

3. Nadine Brozan, "More Teenagers Are Pregnant Despite Rise in Contraception," *New York Times*, 12 March 1981, C1.

4. Armand Nicholi II, "Absent Parents, Troubled Children," *Pastoral Renewal*, May 1980, 89.

5. *United Methodist Reporter,* 8, No. 46 (1980), 3.

6. Olga Fairfax, *United Methodists for Life* Newsletter, 1980.

7. "Children, Sex Pushers and You: A Time for Action," *Growing Parent,* June 1981.

8. Walter Isaacson, "The Battle over Abortion," *Time,* 6 April 1981, 26.

9. Richard Stiller, *The Love Bugs* (New York: Thomas Nelson, 1974), 81.

10. CBS, "60 Minutes," 2 August 1981.

11. Safran, 155.

12. Peter Goldman and Lucille Beachy, *Newsweek,* July 21, 1986, 38-50.

13. Henri Nouwen, *Intimacy* (Notre Dame: Fides Publishers, 1969), 31-32.

14. See the 11th Annual "Who's Who among American High School Students" survey. It revealed that of the top 5 percent of 1980 U.S. high school graduates, 76 percent had not had sexual intercourse and 87 percent desired a traditional marriage.

15. *Linacre Quarterly.* See also statistics compiled in the February 1981 *Phyllis Schlafly Report* from Swedish and U.S. studies correlating the rise in venereal disease and other sex-related problems with the advent and rise of compulsory sex education in public schools.

16. "The Great Orgasmic Robbery," published by the Tepper Rocky Mountain Planned Parenthood of Denver, Colo.

17. S. Gordon, "Ten Heavy Facts about Sex" comic book (Syracuse: Ed-U Press, 1975).

CHAPTER 16.—*Cheaters Never Prosper, or How Adult Is Adultery?*

1. Elaine Denholtz, "All about Eve," *Ashtabula Star Beacon, Family Weekly,* 2 Oct. 1983, 4.

2. Ibid.

CHAPTER 17.—*Abortion: The Hidden Holocaust*

1. John Tippis, "The Challenge to Be Pro Life" (Pro Life Education,

Inc., P. O. Box 30815, Santa Barbara, CA 93105, 3rd ed., 1978).

2. M. and A. Wynn, "Some Consequences of Induced Abortions to Children Born Subsequently," *Marriage and Family Newsletter,* 4, No. 234 (1973). See also Dr. Jack Willke's *Handbook on Abortion* (Cincinnati: Hayes Publishing, 1975), 47.

3. Willke, 47.

4. The definition of salvation used here is a summary from *Baker's Dictionary of Theology,* 469-470.

CHAPTER 18.—*Gay Agony: The Truth about Homosexuality*

1. Enrique T. Rueda, *The Homosexual Network* (Old Greenwich, Conn.: Devin Adair, 1982), 240.

2. Ibid, 242.

3. Ibid, 243.

4. Tim LaHaye, *What Everyone Should Know about Homosexuality* (Wheaton, Ill.: Tyndale House, 1978), 63.

5. Williams, 27, n. 23.

6. LaHaye, 75.

7. Ibid, 71-72.

8. Charles W. Keysor, ed., *What You Should Know about Homosexuality* (Grand Rapids: Zondervan, 1979), 204, n. 33; quoting David F. Busby, "Sexual Deviations: A Psychiatric Overview" in *Proceedings of the Fourteenth Annual Convention of the Christian Association for Psychological Studies* (April 1967), 55-60.

9. Ibid, 147, n. 3: W. J. Gadpaille, "Research into the Physiology of Maleness and Femaleness," *Archives of General Psychiatry* 26 (1973), 193.

10. Leonard LeSourd, ed., *Healing for the Homosexual* (Oklahoma City: Presbyterian Charismatic Communion, 1978), 20-21.

11. Ibid, 30-31.

12. Ibid, 21.

13. LaHaye, 65-92.

14. Williams, 31, n. 48.

15. Kay Oliver and Wayne Christianson, "Unhappily Gay: From the Closet to the Front Page," *Moody Monthly,* January 1978, 64.

16. Keysor, 198, n. 25: *Eternity,* February 1978, 12.

17. LaHaye, 42: quoting Murray Norris, "There's Nothing Gay about Homosexuality," *Christian Family Renewal Newsletter,* Box 73, Clovis, Calif.

18. LaHaye, 39.

19. Montagu, 65.

20. Rueda, 51-56.

21. LaHaye, 42.

22. Ibid, n. 12.
23. Ibid, 50, n. 17; quoting Daniel Cappon *Toward an Understanding of Homosexuality* (Englewood Cliffs, N.J.: Prentice-Hall, 1968), 40.
24. Rueda, 259, 261.
25. Source unknown.
26. Rueda, 246.
27. "Where the Spirit of the Lord Is," *New Covenant* (October 1978), 16.
28. Ibid.
29. Ibid, 18.
30. Williams, 34, n. 70.
31. *New Covenant*, 17-18.
32. M. Scott Peck, *The Road Less Traveled* (New York: Simon and Schuster, 1978), 175.
33. John Knox, "Romans," *The Interpreter's Bible* (Nashville: Abingdon Press, 1954), 9, 401.
34. R. C. H. Lenski, *The Interpretation of St. Paul's Epistle to the Romans* (Columbus, Ohio: Wartburg Press, 1945), 109ff.
35. Rousas John Rushdonny, *The Institutes of Biblical Law* (Craig Press, 1973), 392.

CHAPTER 19.—*A Potpourri of Difficult Questions and Answers*

1. Charlie and Martha Shedd, *Celebration in the Bedroom* (Waco, Tex.: Word Books, 1981), 21-22.
2. Ibid, 22.
3. Ibid, 115.
4. Cory Servaas, M.D., "Hemorrhoids and Other Homosexual Side Effects," *Saturday Evening Post*, April 1986, 108.
5. Cf. *TDNT*, VI, 579-95.
6. J. C. Espinosa, M.D., *Birth Control: Why Are They Lying to Women?* (New York: Vantage Press, 1980), 27.
7. *Webster's New University Dictionary*, Unabridged 2nd ed. (New World Dictionaries, Simon and Schuster, 1983), 1594.
8. Ibid, 1106.
9. S. I. McMillen, M.D., *None of These Diseases* (Old Tappan, N.J.: Fleming H. Revell, 1963), 12-16.

INDEX

PERMISSIONS

The author wishes to acknowledge the following publications and publishers for material quoted in this book:

A Theology of Love by Mildred Wynkoop. Used by permission of the Nazarene Publishing House.

Baker's Dictionary of Theology, Everett Harrison, ed. Used by permission of Baker Book House.

Celebration in the Bedroom by Charlie and Martha Shedd. Used by permission of Word Books.

Clowning in Rome by Henri Nouwen. Used by permission of Doubleday and Co., Inc.

God Calling by A. J. Russell, ed. Used by permission of Dodd, Mead and Co., Inc.

The Christian Family by Larry Christianson. Copyright 1972 by Bethany House Publishers, Minneapolis, MN 55438.

The Homosexual Network by Enrique T. Rueda. Permission to reprint granted by the Devin-Adair Publishers. Copyright 1982 by the Free Congress Research and Education Foundation, Inc.

The Institutes of Biblical Law by Rousas John Rushdonny. Used by permission of Craig Press.

Love and Will by Rollo May. Used by permission of W. W. Norton & Company, Inc.

The Love Command in the New Testament by Victor Paul Furnish. Used by permission of Abingdon Press.

Pastoral Renewal material reprinted with permission from *Pastoral Renewal*, a journal for Christian leaders, P.O. Box 8617, Ann Arbor, MI 48107.

The Prophet by Kahlil Gibran. Used by permission of Alfred A. Knopf, Inc.

"Sex without Love" by Randy Frame. Copyright 1983 by *Christianity Today* and used by permission.

The Theological Dictionary of the New Testament. Used by permission of William B. Eerdmans Publishing Co.

What Everyone Should Know about Homosexuality by Tim LaHaye. Used by permission of Tyndale House Publishers.

What You Should Know about Homosexuality by Charles W. Keysor.